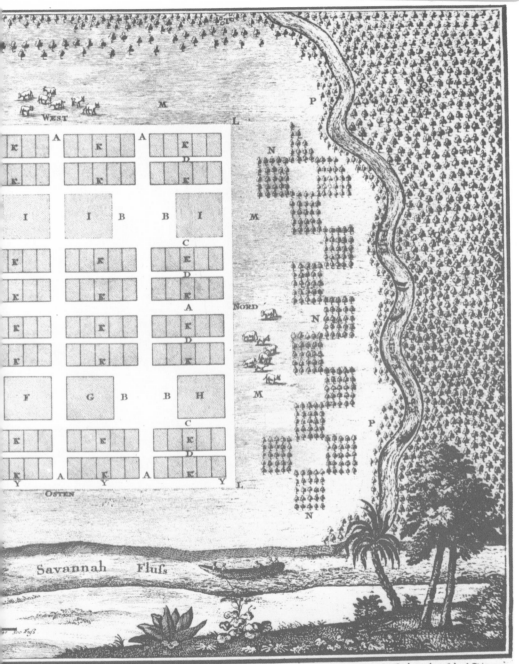

Detailed Reports on the
Salzburger Emigrants
Who Settled in America . . .
Edited by Samuel Urlsperger

DATE DUE

1734   1984

250TH ANNIVERSARY
OF THE SALZBURGERS ARRIVAL

THIS STONE IS DEDICATED TO THE MEMORY OF OUR ANCESTORS THE
GEORGIA SALZBURGERS WHO EMIGRATED FROM GERMANY AND AUSTRIA
IN PURSUIT OF RELIGIOUS FREEDOM LANDING IN SAVANNAH 1734
SOME OF THEIR DESCENDANTS MIGRATED TO THIS AREA MID 1800
AND ARE LAID TO REST HERE. THESE BRAVE AND INDUSTRIOUS
PEOPLE CARVED OUT A NEW WAY OF LIFE UNDER SEVERE ADVERSITIES
REMAINING PIOUS IN THEIR WORSHIP TO GOD AND SERVICE TO COUNTRY.

ERECTED 1984 BY JOHN VERNON HINELY, PRESIDENT, GEORGIA SALZBURGER
SOCIETY–7TH GREAT GRANDSON OF EMIGRANT JOHN HEINLE.

MONUMENT COMMEMORATING THE EARLY SALZBURGERS
BURIED IN THE DASHER CEMETERY IN SOUTHERN GEORGIA.

Detailed Reports on the Salzburger Emigrants Who Settled in America . . .

Edited by Samuel Urlsperger

VOLUME TEN, 1743

Translated by
DON SAVELLE
GEORGE FENWICK JONES

Edited by
GEORGE FENWICK JONES

THE UNIVERSITY OF GEORGIA PRESS
ATHENS AND LONDON

The paper in this book meets the guidelines for permanence
and durability of the Committee on Production Guidelines for
Book Longevity of the Council on Library Resources.

Printed in the United States of America

92 91 90 89 88   5 4 3 2 1

Library of Congress Cataloging in Publication Data

(Revised for vol. 10)

Urlsperger, Samuel, 1685–1772.
    Detailed reports on the Salzburger emigrants who settled in America.

    (Wormsloe Foundation. Publications, no. 9–)
    Vol. 6 translated and edited by George Fenwick Jones and Renate Wilson.
    Vols. 7– translated and edited by George Fenwick Jones and Don
Savelle.
    Vol. 8 translated by Maria Magdalena Hoffmann-Loerzer, Renate Wilson,
and George Fenwick Jones.
    Translation of Ausführliche Nachricht von den saltzburgischen
Emigranten, die sich in America niedergelassen haben.
    Vols. 1–5 issued in series: Publications (Wormsloe Foundation)
    Includes bibliographical references and indexes.
    Contents: v. 1. 1733–1734—[etc.]—v. 8. 1741—   —v. 10. 1743.
    1. Salzburgers—Georgia—History—Sources. 2. German Americans—
Georgia—History—Sources. 3. Lutherans—Georgia—History—Sources. 4.
Ebenezer (Ga.)—History—Sources. 5. Georgia—History—Colonial period.
ca. 1600–1775—Sources. 6. Stockbridge Indians—Missions—History—
Sources. 7. Indians of North America—Georgia—Missions—History—
Sources. I. Jones, George Fenwick, 1916–   . II. Wilson, Renate,
1930–   . III. Savelle, Don. IV. Title. V. Series. VI. Series: Publications
(Wormsloe Foundation); v. 9, etc.
F295.S1U813   975.8'00431   67-27137
ISBN 0-8203-1050-6 (alk. paper) (v. 10)

British Library Cataloging in Publication Data available

Volumes 1–5 were published as part of the Wormsloe Foundation
Publications series.

Contents

Introduction by
George Fenwick Jones

vii

Diary for the Year 1743

1

Appendix I
Hymns Sung in 1743

129

Appendix II
German-speaking Transports to Georgia

131

Notes

169

Index

177

Introduction

The following five paragraphs are taken from the introduction to the previous volume of this series and therefore should be skipped by those who have already read it or who are otherwise familiar with the history of the Georgia Salzburgers. For those who come new to the field, the following resumé should suffice.[1] When the Lutherans were expelled from Salzburg in 1731, not all the exiles went to East Prussia and other Protestant lands in Europe: a small number, some two hundred, were taken to the colony of Georgia, then in its second year. Georgia, the last of Britain's thirteen North American colonies, was founded according to the grandiose schemes of a group of benevolent gentlemen in London, called the Trustees, who wished to provide homes for impoverished Englishmen and persecuted foreign Protestants, to protect the more northerly colonies from the Spaniards in Florida, and to provide raw materials for English industry.

The first Salzburger transport, or traveling party, consisted of recent exiles who had been recruited in and around Augsburg, a Swabian city just north of Salzburg. This group arrived in Georgia in 1734 and settled some twenty-five miles northwest of Savannah, where they founded a settlement which they named Ebenezer. By the time the second transport arrived a year later, it had been discovered that the land that had been chosen was sterile and that the stream on which it was built, Ebenezer Creek, was unnavigable. When a third transport arrived in 1736, composed mostly of Upper Austrian exiles, the survivors at Ebenezer joined them on the Red Bluff on the Savannah River, bringing the name of the earlier settlement with them. The original site, which became the Trustees' cowpen or cattle ranch, was henceforth called Old Ebenezer.

A fourth and last transport, consisting of Salzburger exiles who had been sojourning in Augsburg and other Swabian cities, arrived in 1741. The Salzburgers were joined by Swiss and Palatine settlers from Purysburg, a Swiss settlement a short way down the Savannah River on the Carolina side, and also by some Palatine servants donated by the Trustees. Not finding enough fertile land on the Red Bluff, many Salzburgers moved their plantations to an area along Abercorn Creek where the lowland was flooded and enriched each winter by the Savannah River. This explains the terms "the town" and "the plantations." After some gristmills and sawmills were built on Abercorn Creek, it was usually called the Mill River *(Mühl-Fluss)*.

Despite appalling sickness and mortality and the hardships incident to settlement in a wilderness, the Salzburgers were the most successful community in Georgia. This relative success was largely due to the skill, devotion, and diligence of their spiritual leader, Johann Martin Boltzius, the author of most of these reports. This young divine had been trained at the University of Halle in eastern Germany and had taught in that city at the Francke Foundation, a charitable institution that was to have great influence on the development of Ebenezer. Although Boltzius was at heart a minister, his secular responsibilities in Georgia moulded him into a skilful administrator, economist, and diplomat. A few of the reports were written by Boltzius' admiring younger colleague, Israel Christian Gronau, who officiated whenever Boltzius was away in Savannah or elsewhere.

Boltzius' journals were edited contemporaneously by Samuel Urlsperger, the Senior of the Lutheran clergy in Augsburg. Comparison of the original manuscripts surviving in Halle with Urlsperger's published edition shows that he took considerable liberty in deleting unpleasant reports and suppressing proper names, which he replaces with N. or N.N. The original documents for 1743 no longer exist, so there is no way to know how much Urlsperger changed or deleted; but there is reason to believe that Boltzius made an entry for every day, as he had been instructed to, and that Urlsperger made major deletions both for diplomatic and for economic reasons. In some cases he simply consolidated the material for two or more days into one. Urlsperger's deletions are very illogical: he often deletes a name in one passage even though it appears in another and can be easily recognized. For example, he deletes the name of a sinful town immediately after discussing Purysburg; and, when the

Schwartzwälder child dies, the blame is put on N., who can be none other than its father.

Strangers to the Pietists' otherworldly value system should be reminded that they gave deeper meanings to many common words. For example, "misery" (*Elend*) meant "sin," it being an alienation from God; and wealthy people were in the greatest danger of living in misery. "Indolent" (*träge*) meant lax in prayer and could therefore be applied to a man who spent his whole day in chopping and plowing. All sicknesses were "salutary"; for, although harmful for the body, they were wholesome for the soul by humbling it and making it dependent on the merits of Christ.

Unfortunately, because Urslperger shortened or deleted so many entries, these later volumes are less dependable for statistical purpose. For example, in the surviving entries for the year 1742 Boltzius reported only fifteen deaths, yet in the first entry of 1743 he summarizes that twenty-five people had died during the previous year.

Less tumultous than 1742, the year of the Spanish Invasion, and less tragic with regard to sickness and death, the year 1743 was less noteworthy; yet there was considerable progress in agriculture, cattle raising, and the new enterprise in viticulture and sericulture. Perhaps the greatest advance was in the introduction of the plow, which had been neglected as long as the ground was full of roots and the Salzburgers lacked horses. Seeing how much energy the Salzburgers were expending in tilling their fields with the hoe, Boltzius gradually persuaded them to invest in plows and horses, which enabled them to grow "German" crops such as wheat, barley, rye, and oats in place of just corn, rice, and beans. He failed, however, in persuading them to cultivate the piney lands, which he was sure would yield abundantly if only properly manured. In this belief he was wrong.

The beginnings made at this time in growing grapevines led to little, and gradually the effort petered out. The silk industry, on the other hand, continued progressing and became for a short time the chief cash crop, but only as long as the Trustees subsidized it. Cattle raising, which had been the most successful undertaking. suffered a serious setback when the cattle disease, called "blackwater" by the English, reached Ebenezer after plaguing the neighboring areas for more than a year. To judge by the complaints, it would almost seem that the Salzburgers regretted the mortality among their cattle as much as that among their children. Their cattle were their chief support, joy, and measure of their status and self-esteem.

In addition to greater productivity, the Salzburgers distinguished themselves in construction, both in replacing their huts with cottages and in undertaking communal projects, such as repair of Jerusalem Church, the construction of Zion Church on the plantations, and work on the all-important mill. While such mundane toil is seldom mentioned by historians, it was the basis of our national expansion.

During the uneventful year 1743 the Salzburgers were busy consolidating their position and enhancing their reputation as the most industrious element in the colony. By clearing the forests and building the first successful gristmills and sawmills, they were preparing the way for new arrivals from the Palatinate, Wurttemberg, and German Switzerland. These newcomers conformed to the ways of the earlier settlers, intermarried with them, and formed a close-knit religious community, which held together until the Revolution, by which time all nearby land was taken up and younger sons had to look elsewhere to establish their farms. Most of those who left Ebenezer moved to North Georgia and the Carolina frontier; but some of them moved southwards as soon as the Creek Indians ceded their lands.

Hardly more than a century after their first arrival in Georgia enough of the Salzburgers reached the extreme south of Georgia to maintain their identity, as is evidenced by the cemetary at Dasher, a town some nine miles south of Valdosta and not far from the Florida line. In this cemetary one finds stones to the Dashers, Flerls, Hinelys, Wizenbackers, and other Salzburger families. These settlers are commemorated by a handsome stone, illustrated on the frontispiece of this volume, on which is written:

DASHER, GA.
1734   1984
250th ANNIVERSARY

THIS STONE IS DEDICATED TO THE MEMORY OF OUR ANCESTORS, THE GEORGIA SALZBURGERS WHO EMIGRATED FROM GERMANY AND AUSTRIA IN PURSUIT OF RELIGIOUS FREEDOM, LANDING AT SAVANNAH 1734. SOME OF THEIR DESCENDANTS MIGRATED TO THIS AREA MID 1800 AND ARE LAID TO REST HERE. THESE BRAVE AND INDUSTRIOUS PEOPLE CARVED OUT A NEW WAY OF LIFE UNDER SEVERE ADVERSITIES, REMAINING PIOUS IN THEIR WORSHIP TO GOD AND SERVICE TO COUNTRY.

ERECTED 1984 BY JOHN VERNON HINELY, PRESIDENT, GEORGIA SALZBURGER SOCIETY—THE 7th GREAT GRANDSON OF EMIGRANT JOHN HINELY.

In addition to erecting this monument of stone, J. Vernon Hinely and his wife, Bonnie L. Hinely, have also dedicated another monument to the Salzburgers, namely this volume of the *Detailed Reports*.

Detailed Reports on the
Salzburger Emigrants
Who Settled in America . . .
Edited by Samuel Urlsperger

In the Name of Jesus, Amen

DIARY FOR THE YEAR 1743

JANUARY

Saturday, New Year's Day. Yesterday evening at the close of the old year we held a regular prayer hour in which we bent our knees before our reconciled Father in Jesus' name. We humbly asked Him to forgive us our omission of the good and commission of evil in thoughts, works, and deeds; we praised Him for all the spiritual and physical benefactions heretofore rendered to us and implored Him for new grace for a right serious Christian way of life. Today our merciful Lord strengthened us noticeably for expounding His sweet gospel for us and our parishioners and encouraging us amongst ourselves to come to Christ Himself. He is the living source from whom many thousands have already drawn grace upon grace for the beginning and progress of their Christianity.

Because it is customary to read aloud on New Year's Day the number of children born as well as the persons who married and the persons who died, we did this today. In the previous one thousand seven hundred and forty second year eleven children were born of whom seven are still living. Nine couples, members of the Ebenezer congregation, were married. Twenty four persons, to wit fourteen adults and ten children, died.[1] From the beginning till now in the Ebenezer congregation one hundred children have been born, one hundred twelve persons have died, and fifty-seven couples have been married. May God grant that this year all those still lacking true conversion sincerely convert to God so that even if this year, as in the previous one, some may be called to eternity, they may help to increase not hell but the church triumphant!

Sunday, the 2nd of January. Theobald Kieffer's wife /Maria/ and her mother /Anna Margaretha/, both long sick, were also at public divine services yesterday and today, although they are still very feeble and they find sitting, moving, and listening rather difficult. The love and desire for the word of God drew them here, for the young Kieffer always brought something edifying home to them from church. He was, however, not able to explain it to them as God had brought it to his heart; nonetheless by means of his explanation and exposition he stimulated their appetite for the benevolent word of God.

Monday, the 3rd of January. Theobald Kieffer's helpmeet / Maria/, of whose honest, desirous attitude for the wise, pure milk we reported somewhat yesterday, had hardly gotten home to her plantation last evening when our dear Lord delivered her of her burden and presented her a healthy and well-formed little son. God gave her the grace so that not only was she edified and refreshed by His sweet gospel during her lying-in but also she heard something of yesterday's gospel on the baptism of the Lord Jesus, which brought much joy to her, her mother and her husband in the current circumstances. We learned among other things that a true Christian, who has renewed his baptismal convenant by means of true conversion, may boast that in his tender childhood he received the same thing which the Lord Jesus, our Leader, also received, to wit, holy baptism. Since remarkable, mysterious things occurred at His baptism, God also manifested the abundance of His grace and kindness at our own and our children's baptisms; for heaven opened up, the Holy Spirit poured out upon us abundantly, and we were made sons and daughters of God for the sake of Christ. He has all of His favor in us, hence we would not only attach great importance to the holy baptism but also recognize the great treasure in the Christian children and tell them often many beautiful things therefrom, and accustom them to valuing Him above all else.

N. had me called to his place because he has been ill since his marriage. He had his wife's two children in front of his bed and was seeking to impart something good to them. When I stepped up to him in his hut he had the children go out and acknowledged that God was causing his sins to fall heavily on his conscience, in that his whole life long he had sinned grievously against God, his parents, friends, his wife, and others. He said he had had a terrifying dream: his late wife, with whom he had gotten along very badly, was always standing before him, as it were, and it seemed terrible to him whenever he considered that couples once married should be forever separated from one another if they both had not lived in a Christian manner and died blessedly. His sins were oppressing him; they drew many sighs and prayers from him day and night, but nonetheless he hoped, he said, that God would also accept him, great sinner, in grace. If he should die, he said, he desired that all his things be left to his present wife and that he be buried next to his pious former wife in the cemetery on the plantations. I told him he should be concerned not simply for his body but primarily for his soul, and that now by means of true penitence he might lay such a foundation that, if he should recover, people would be able to recognize the truth of his penitence from his piety. He was greatly concerned for the soul of his wife and children, and it appeared to me that his penitence and conversion were genuine. I believe that our dear Lord is now beginning to view and hear the past prayers and tears of his late wife for him in grace for the sake of Christ.

Tuesday, the 4th of January. Schwartzwälder, a German servant of the Lord Trustees in Old Ebenezer, has now become free along with his children. He wishes to take a plantation at our place, for which purpose he has gotten permission from us. Today he rode to Savannah to obtain the consent of the authorities there for it. He is an honest man and has showed himself faithful in his time of service and has been diligent in coming regularly to our divine services. We are happy to receive proper people amongst us, and we confer upon them every possible advantage. It is a quite great physical benefaction that the Lord Trustees not only give their German servants who have served them five years money for house and farm implements and also a year's daily allowance but also liberate all their children, who would have had quite a long time to serve.[2] They demonstrate thereby that they seek only the best for the people.

Thursday, the 6th of January. Today we celebrated the Feast of the Epiphany, for which already yesterday evening in the prayer hour we sought to prepare ourselves by word and prayer. Since in the Christian church from ages past other feast days are decreed for the solemn, grateful remembrance of the great benefactions, it is most just that we also not let this feast of the Epiphany fall into disuse as happens here completely in this country. For what good indeed would the birth, passion, death, resurrection, and ascension of Christ, etc. do us if we, who are heathens by race, were not brought to the community of the Christian church and could not share in the sermon on Christ and His merited grace. My dear colleague had as text the beautiful 117th Psalm, so like the New Testament. He sought to extol the grace and truth that we now have from Christ and in which not just a few peoples but all heathens and peoples should share, and to glorify this grace and truth to our parishioners.

In the morning our subject was the gospel, the occasion being the important words of the Lord Jesus, John 5:39, on the main content and proper use of Holy Scripture, when young and old together were shown what a great benefaction of God it was that not only had God's word been translated into our German tongue but also that our parishioners are so abundantly provided with Bibles and New Testaments. For this great and quite undeserved benefaction we justly glorify our dear Lord and we should pray zealously for our benefactors in Europe who have been helpful therein with generous gifts so that the Father in heaven may compensate them for such loving gifts with spiritual, physical, and eternal blessings.

Saturday, the 8th of January. Carl Flerl's wife had gotten fever while in childbed; and, because the medicines from Halle had formerly done her much good, she asked me for a few doses, which quickly had a good effect with her and her little child. She was at my house this morning and could not find words enough to express her grateful feeling regarding it. When we talked of the spiritual pilgrims who had to help themselves in every possible way on their travels and we came to the Salzburg emigrants, she marveled at and praised God for the kindness He had showed her and other Salzburgers on the journey and here. She said God had saved her from the claws of the enemies,[3] and wherever she looked she felt the pure blessings of God which were poured out abundantly over great and lowly.

Sunday, the 9th of January. Because someone told me yesterday a few edifying details of Mrs. Bacher's illness, my spirit was powerfully moved to ride out yesterday afternoon to edify myself from the grace which she had again experienced; and our dear Lord presented me here with so much pleasure and edification that I could quite noticeably feel His gracious presence. She bore witness, in great poverty of spirit, to the good the Lord had shown her in her difficult sick-bed. She was already certain of God's grace in Christ; but, when the feeling of it sometimes became lost again, our loving Savior gave it to her once more now so that she sensed not a sensual joy but rather a joy resting deeply in her heart, a joy which flowed from peace and conciliation. She made much of the fact that on the journey and here in this country God had done her much spiritual and physical good by means of Christian instruments and benefactors, and she wished to be able to write so that she could express in writing the condition of her heart and gratitude. When she heard that I was now writing to the benefactors she requested that I also write heartfelt good wishes to them for their sake, and amongst other things this, too, which we find in the hymn *Du meiner Augen-Licht*, "Yes, yes, I shall gladly take up the cross on these shoulders and subject my neck to the gentle yoke, to follow my bright morning-star. Well then, ye worldly desires must die, thou hard hard sense of vanity, thou love of gain, leave this house of my heart. Go thy ways."

We spoke of faith a good deal with one another, and we were in the same spirit as one who knows not from hearsay how things appear but rather is right at home, so to speak, and recognizes every corner in the house and what belongs in it. Likewise, we agreed that the witness of the Holy Spirit and the relationship to it that one desires can be described with words as little as being born again; rather, it must be experienced. The two daughters were heartily admonished about the content of the verse Matthew 3:12, not, indeed, to be Christians of chaff and hulls on the threshing floor of Christ, Christians who are carried off by each and every wind of lust and enticement and are finally burned up with eternal fire, but rather to become for once Christians of good wheat and kernel. When it comes to threshing and God strikes out at the people with cross and affliction, then the wheat and chaff reveal and separate themselves.

Monday, the 10th of January. Col. Stephens is quite well satisfied that some of the Lord Trustees' servants are settling at our place. He wishes to have the same assistance granted to them that others enjoy, and herewith the calumny of a few Germans in Savannah collapses; the rumor was spreading that those Germans who take land in Ebenezer would get no assistance.

Wednesday, the 12th of January. Last evening I learned that the old N. woman had been confined to bed, hence I visited her this morning. During the conversation, which dealt with the Godpleasing preparation for blessed eternity, she asked me the meaning of "denying oneself." I could do no better than to explain it to her with Paul's words and example in Philippians 3:4-14, which passage I read aloud to her and applied constantly to her situation. She still has much self righteousness and self-piety and puts her trust in the means of salvation and in her reputable demeanor, which makes a great obstacle for her true conversion.[4] I also told her various things about the important verse "To open their eyes, and to turn them from darkness," and I recommended the hymns *Erleucht' mich, Herr, mein Licht!* etc. and *Du sagst, ich bin ein Christ* etc., *Treuer Vater, deine Liebe*, etc.

Saturday, the 15th of January. Mrs. N. has become seriously ill; and, when I visited her, I sought diligently to lead her to the penitent recognition of her sin and peril. When I presented to her her unfaithfulness towards the grace of the Holy Spirit, which she often felt powerfully when she used the means, and when I also reminded her of her good beginning to conversion in her earlier perilous illness, she began in her great weakness to pray, so powerfully and properly, with raised hands, that it rejoiced my heart. She accused herself strongly, and took her refuge in the most moving manner in the mercy of God in Christ; and she promised through the assistance of the holy spirit to become and to remain faithful to the Lord Jesus.

Sunday, the 16th of January. The Englishman from Old Ebenezer had sent his boy on horseback to collect a small debt for the cattle search. When I asked him why he had come here on Sunday for that, he answered that they did not know today was Sunday, rather they were under the impression it was Saturday. They live quite from hand to mouth and pay no heed to the fourth commandment,[5] hence there is blessing nowhere, rather everywhere is accursed. This afternoon the fourth commandment was expounded for us and impressed on us according to its evangelical contents. The late Luther hit it quite beautifully when he rhymed as follows: "You should drop your work so that God can work in you."[6]

Tuesday, the 18th of January. I have much pleasure in conversation and prayer with Mrs. Arnsdorf's eldest daughter Sophy. She is a patient, and when God began His good work in her formerly I was hoping He would wish to make her one of the really select on the occasion of the current illness, through the blood of Christ. She was amongst the orphan children at the time Magdalena Haberfehner went to joyous eternity with the beautiful verse "I will be glad in the Lord, and my soul is joyful," of which I reminded her.

Thursday, the 20th of January. R.S. has been greatly refreshed by the 15th chapter of Luke, and S.R. attested that he was quite certain of the remission of his sins for the sake of Christ; but, he said, his present chastisement through sickness was causing him distress,[7] for in his youth he had gotten into a good deal of trouble. God was now showing him this and it was very pleasing to him. He knows from the stories we have contemplated till now that our dear Lord has also always been behind his family after their penitence and their conversion through punishment.

Friday, the 21st of January. Morning and afternoon I visited some of our sick little sheep on their plantations. They are likely lying on the loving shoulders of the Lord Jesus; and, if they should die, they would be delivered to the eternal sheepfold where the holy lambs are. I made this day Friday and what happened on it through Christ's bitter passion profitable to some of them with the beautiful words: "Thou hast wearied me with thine iniquities," also, "Behold, thy king cometh into thee. He is just and having salvation."

Theobald Kieffer's wife /Maria/ told me that her husband, at her request, had calculated how long they had been ill one after another. It came to 34 weeks. They added, praising God, that the long time had seemed very short to them nonetheless. I said only retrospectively would they see how good it was meant to be. He has been perilously ill with stitches in his side but our dear Lord so far has blessed in him the medicine from Halle. The couple and the mother were very affectionate and intimate together, and their expression impressed me so much that I could feel that the Lord was amongst them, etc.

Mrs. N. showed me in her garden very large, fat turnips and black radishes that were simply astounding. A couple of people could eat from just one of them till they were satisfied. Such blessings encourage her to apply herself more to raising vegetables, which has brought her, as a widow, something for her necessary expenditures. To be sure, the frequent illnesses hinder many in their necessary physical labor; but for those who conform to God's order the profit from it is greater than the loss. And for the Lord it is an easy thing also to free us from the illnesses when His time shall come.

Monday the 24th of January. All our patients whom I visited morning and afternoon are beginning to improve and seem now to be out of danger, as perilous as it looked for a few in the beginning. And I was told exactly the same thing of a few others whom I was not able to visit. We were very much gladdened for this reason at the recovery of some of them and we thank God for it because they still have the time of grace most necessary for their true conversion and preparation for eternity, about which I could not refrain from talking to them. Those who promised much good while confined to bed are being reminded to make true their word and good resolution by means of His grace. From their way of life after their illness they will be able to perceive whether their remorse on their sick-bed was a true one effected by God or a remorse and resolution forced out by fear of hell. Hence they will also be able to tell whether their faith was a true faith and whether, if they had died with it, they would have been able to pass before Christ's seat of judgment.

That the penitence of many people on their sick-bed is only human work and hypocrisy is betrayed by their way of life following recovery. For, if their misery and peril were disclosed to them by the punitive office of the Holy Spirit and if a real shame and hatred about and towards sin were effected in them and a real esteem for reconciliation through Christ and a faithful hunger and thirst for Him, nonetheless this change of heart and the good tree planted therein would have to manifest themselves in good fruit.

Wednesday, the 26th of January. As I was aware that

Sanftleben had hardly harvested a bushel of corn because of illness and other occurrences, I offered to send him three shillings
for two bushels of corn. But he gave me the unexpected answer
that he had no lack thereof, for the people in the congregation
had sent him upwards of thirteen bushels.

Friday, the 28th of January. Mrs. Schweighoffer is now feeling
very great weakness in her body, and every day she expects her
dissolution and passage from this to a better life through temporal death. She was still at my house prior to my departure, and
my going seemed very bitter to her. She had us write down how
her cattle and little money should be distributed amongst her
three children, being governed in this matter precisely according to the prescription of her late husband. The best depositum
and legacy she is leaving behind for her children is a zealous,
constant prayer for them and a very beautiful example of true
piety. It is to be hoped that even after her death it will be blessed
in them, although till now she has still not had the joy of seeing
her children as truly faithful ones in the arms of Jesus and leaving them behind in them, as it were.

When I was with her I often mentioned to her the words of
that pious bishop who often consoled the pious Monica on account of her Augustine, that children of so many tears and
prayers cannot be lost. I left behind with her the following little
verse along with the appended verses on a printed note: Isaiah
51:11 "Therefore the redeemed of the Lord shall return, and
come with singing unto Zion; and everlasting joy shall be upon
their head: they shall obtain gladness and joy; and sorrow and
mourning shall flee away." John 16:22. Also, "My God will treat
me there with everlasting joy. My cross, beknownst to me and
Him, will turn to heavenly bliss. There my tears will naught but
wine become, my trembling just pure bliss. This I know, so help
me God. Amen."[8]

FEBRUARY

Tuesday, the 1st of February. When we observed the important words of David to his son Solomon, I Chronicles 23:9, we
were reminded that it was God's purpose that we, too, use this
time of peace properly, as did Solomon, for the edification of the

spiritual temple of God, as we had the example of the first Christians before us, Acts 9:31. For my parishioners I once more emphasized the important pronouncement of God in Psalm 81:4ff. "But my people would not hearken," etc. and I reminded them of the words at 2 Samuel 24:1 "And again the anger of the Lord was kindled," etc. We have already heard once the grim anger of the Lord from afar; we have to stand on our guard so that it is not kindled again. It is known from the story what finally happened to King Solomon when he grew disobedient to the Lord and made himself like the heathens through idolatry: God raised up adversaries against him, and this stands as a warning to us.

Wednesday, the 2nd of February. It is now the time for planting the new wine grapes. I am also having that done on the piece of land near my house which I had someone dig and prepare last year for wine grape planting. The whole plot includes 425 vines which stand four feet from one another. I need very few indeed of the clippings from Col. Stephens because I have more than I need of the vines which grew in my garden last year. For I do not wish to overextend myself. It turned out that, when cut down, my vines had much of their wood frozen. This happened because of the very cold wind, because previously they were green and healthy. I also expected confidently to grow them the first year over six feet, also often to leave two to three shoots standing on one root when one would have been enough, and each should have been only four feet long in the first year, then the wood would be quite hard and strong.

Friday, the 4th of February. A woman from the plantations told me very anxiously that, shortly before, she had fallen into disunity with her husband, for which she may herself have given the opportunity. She is serious and zealous in her Christianity but her husband is indolent towards what is good and carries out the external divine services in church and at home just out of habit. Because she would like now to save her husband's soul, she often speaks to him but does it more in an anxious manner than with gentle and quiet spirit, as is required of the female sex, I Peter 3:1, ff. When chastised by the Holy Spirit she easily became aware that she was causing harm; and she was so downcast by it that she fell into bodily weakness and was hindered in attending the public divine services, so that it seemed to her that she was unworthy of the word of God to which she had not been quite obedient, etc. I instructed her to avoid both extremes, and neither to be silent at all her husband's bad behavior nor fly into him with blustering and hard words, but rather to take the middle path, with the aid of the Holy Spirit. And, since she is horrified on account of her sins and is coming to pay close attention to them, I pointed out to her that she would also have to learn to take joy in, and take comfort in, the Lord Jesus alone and to hasten to the free and open fountain for washing away sin and uncleanliness, with all her filth and uncleanliness.

A second woman near the town has her household burden in her young husband, who wishes to be wiser than the word of God and who knows how to oppose the sermons on penitence, faith, and righteousness with a good deal from the school of the Old Adam. She complained to me about certain special circumstances and requested my counsel and assistance. She has a quite honest attitude. She sees her husband's great peril; she is full of pity for him, she deals very kindly with him and prays zealously for him so that his soul might still be saved. Her behavior towards her husband pleased me very much, and I wished the same tender, quiet, and therewith zealous condition in the proper limits for all pious people, especially those who have a dissimilar spouse at their side. Blame, judgment, and rejection is also otherwise quite common even amongst good souls. How long God has borne us, steered us, and in like manner once more pulled the carriage from the mire into which we drove it and had difficulty with each and every one of His children before He was able to bring that child into His order. One should ponder diligently upon it and follow the method of God and Christ: "Thou shouldst love thy neighbor so that he will enjoy thee as God has had joy of thee."

Monday, the 7th of February. This year the plantations around the long bridge which lie between the city and the mill stream are being occupied. They belong mostly to those people who live in the city and who for the past year have planted the gardens lying nearby. But these are now used up and have been taken over by a kind of grass that is almost impossible to get rid of but which gives very good hay. Therefore the people have been obliged to begin the work on their own plantations, and probably this year the fields around town may be left untilled and used for pasturage and hay. The men have already been busy for the last two weeks splitting rails[1] and providing security for their plantations with a common fence, just as others at the mill stream and Ebenezer River have done. Such mutual, harmonious labor overcomes great difficulties. If each one should make his own fence around his land he would not get along, as we see in so many examples in the country. The purpose and decree of the Lord Trustees was very praiseworthy when, from the beginning, they insisted on mutual labor and assistance in house building and agriculture amongst the inhabitants. It has not been properly understood, however, and selfishness and wilfulness have destroyed this decree.[2]

In the beginning our people, unasked and according to previous Christian consideration, had their plantations divided into three parts. These, therefore, became very long and narrow. Afterwards the authorities in Savannah certified this and now the plantations for the Germans at White Bluff on the Vernon River are divided in the same way, for each landlord can quite comfortably clear trees and bushes from his narrow strip of land and more easily guard the crop from vermin, to his neighbor's advantage and his own profit, and also finish with the fence more easily and quickly. They also dwell closer to one another in this manner in case of need one can assist the other sooner.[3]

The Lord Trustees are having the Germans paid the diet-money with the stipulation that they must labor in the fields on their own plantations.[4] Whoever does not fulfill this stipulation has no share in this benefaction of the diet-money. The monies however are paid out only monthly and they are obliged thereby not only to begin but also diligently to carry on their labor, otherwise many a person would leave his profession and go out into day labor, which brings them more, as it seems, than regular labor in agriculture. It is nonetheless somewhat uncertain, and with their running back and forth they do not lead an orderly life, as we see in many of the old inhabitants. Even the widows of the German people have taken on plantations since they will probably apply a part of the money that they receive over an entire year for tools and provisions and to having the men cut down the trees for them and doing a few other labors.

Tuesday, the 8th of February. Mr. Zübli[5] from Purysburg wrote to me that he is keeping most of his Negroes for only a few more days and that he wishes to divest himself of this burden and change his manner of living according to the direction God is showing. Since some people amongst us need rice, he wishes that they might fetch it from his old plantation during this high water, and that also took place today. Indeed some amongst us have rice left over that they can sell but they lack time to thresh it and make it fit for sale, which takes a lot of time and great labor, since we still have no stamping mills.[6]

The people of the last transport planted almost no rice on account of illness and therefore they had to buy it as well as other provisions. One hundred pounds of good rice costs six shillings sixpence sterling. But the white flour is more than twice as expensive. It seems that Mr. Zübli is becoming more and more aware that the burden with the Negroes is greater than the profit. In addition, there can be no blessing in this unChristian manner of living.[7] It is good when people become wise in time before they get too entangled in harm. Perhaps he is doing it like the husband of Mrs. Montaigut,[8] whose plantation he leased, for fear of the Spaniards. He rid himself of his Negroes, for during time of war especially they are not sure of their lives with them, which is a great misery and in the dominion over them there is at the same time a kind of slavery.

Wednesday, the 9th of February. It appears again this year that the people on the plantations along the Mill River will once more be unable to plant their low-lying land because the deep sections, always dry a few years ago, are almost constantly inundated or at least wet. Hence some of them went back to the dry land that needs manure and is not as good and productive as the land beyond the Mill River. The mill dam is somewhat but not entirely to blame, as already mentioned elsewhere. When Mr. Zübli arrived in the country he bought a plantation of 200 acres on the Savannah River; but, because of the frequent inundations occurring more than previously for two years now, he has been forced to abandon it and has leased another in the middle of the country. It is however quite distant and inconvenient for bringing crops and other things back and forth, especially since the paths are watery and at times almost impassable.

In like manner other people from Purysburg have had to abandon such land for this reason, and some of those have moved to a bountiful region near Port Royal, where, however, they do not get their own land but to a certain extent are vassals of some prominent gentlemen in London, to whom this barony belongs. We have elsewhere reported how it has often gone with young Kieffer on his low-lying plantation across from us in Carolina (it is still somewhat higher than ours by the Mill River). People think in Carolina that if this low-lying land brings a crop just every three years because of inundation it is worth cultivating because it bears almost as much in one year as another would in three. I do not see, however, that this observation is valid, and it certainly does not apply on those plantations where the people are just beginners and otherwise have no regularly dry land like Kieffer's and that of many other people. Because the flooding has persisted so unusually for two years we are guessing that higher up in Indian country another river has torn loose from its banks and passed over into the Savannah River, but we have no certainty of that.

In Surinam the land is also said to be so low-lying, which once induced the English to cede it to the Dutch for New York. The Dutch are accustomed to making dams in their country and they also have the means for it. If our dear Lord grants the means, there will have to be a change with our mill and its dams so that the good and very fruitful soil in the vicinity of the stream can be used. If we could make that land usable, our people would profit greatly with little trouble from agriculture and cattle breeding, with God's blessing. There is no other place in our area as convenient for placing the mill as the place where it now stands.

Thursday, the 10th of February. There is now young grass not only near the city but also a good piece away; the horses and cattle run after it greedily and so we have to look for them with some trouble. It happens every winter that this old grass is burned away. Where such burning takes place in a timely manner there is also, if the cold and the frost do not persist too long, young grass in season. Nonetheless, some areas have to be burned off early in spring because otherwise horses and other beasts would have no grass before the young grass grew back. We in town, like those people in the area of the mill, have no herdsman, hence the cows are driven alone into the forest.[9] Now, on account of the sweet young grass, they wander a long way and the people have great trouble around evening time bringing them together again and home. If the cows stay out a few nights, the people are harmed because of the milk, which is a part of their necessary nourishment. They also like to have those cows near the city which are supposed to get calves at this time. If those cows remain in the woods, the calves are in peril of the wolves, which are very harmful.[10]

We hear quite often that young calves are devoured by bears and wolves. It happens almost every time if the cows with their calves do not remain with the entire herd but rather wander here and there singly or remain in the woods at night. Herdsmen are difficult to get because no one hires out as a servant but rather prefers working for daily wages in the country, which amounts to a lot in a year. There has already been for some time a German man from Purysburg in our congregation working now and again for daily wages.[11] Those who wish to employ him at labor must give him daily good food and 14 pence sterling, which in German money comes out to a half gulden.

Friday, the 11th of February. I found in Rottenberger's house finished cedar wood from which small wooden containers are to be manufactured. I learned at the same time that the man had found such a cedar tree on his own plantation not far from our bridge and had carried it home piecemeal to make some useful containers for some people. They are longer lasting than those being made of common wood. Trees such as those are found otherwise only by the sea in Georgia and Carolina, and I was astounded that we should come across one in our area, too. Our people have roamed the areas hereabouts thoroughly but have nowhere seen cedar trees. It is beautiful red and white flecked, sweet smelling wood, and long lasting. Anyone who can make fence posts from it has a garden fence good for many years; on the other hand other wood rots quite quickly in the ground and in the weather.

I am told that on General Oglethorpe's barony by Palachocolas and likewise in the area of Augusta, there are also many cedar trees that are used very advantageously in construction. They are said, however, not to grow very thick, straight, or tall; and there is, therefore, a great difference between ours and the cedars mentioned in holy scripture. People also cut boards from them. The widest ones I have seen were one foot wide and were offered to me at 2 pence sterling per foot in Savannah. There are a good many cypress trees in swampy and watery areas. They are of uncommon thickness and height and have a soft, easily worked and nonetheless durable wood that is very profitable to use for boats or barges, as also for construction. In house construction in this country there is the inconvenience that one cannot lay a sound foundation because of a dearth of stones, hence one must lay the foundation from resinous pine. To be sure, bricks are to be had for money, but they are expensive because they have to be brought here partly in place of ballast from England, partly from Carolina, Cape Fear, and the northern provinces, partly because the transportation charge from Savannah costs too much. There is sufficient lime and wood in our area, but we lack the resources to set up brick kilns and baking ovens here. In Savannah a similar thing has been tried, also a few years ago in Purysburg, but this arrangement soon ceased because, on account of the excessive daily wages, the expenses were greater than the profits. They are also only baked in the open air beneath an earth covering and hence do not become really hard.

In Savannah and in some places in Carolina one finds in the ground a certain kind of ironstones that at first are soft and easy to cut but that become almost as hard as iron if they lie a while in the open air. They lie quite high in the earth, and if they are dug out a few feet deep then pure sand appears once more. They use these stones in Savannah instead of sills and foundations, and the foundations are of great durability. In our area we have not yet found anything like them. On the shore of the Savannah River between here and Palachocolas there are cliffs, even limestones, that no one is able or wishes to quarry because people and expenses are required for it. In the beginning one helps oneself in construction as well as one can.

Sunday, the 13th of February. Although the cold was severe,

the parishioners gathered as abundantly as in a more comfortable time. Where there is true hunger and thirst for the word of life one does not allow oneself to be kept away either for cold or other circumstances that one can overcome. A lazy and self-satisfied person always knows how to find obstacles and excuses. Both the people and the authorities sometimes have to be satisfied with such excuses, but the day of judgment will make it clear whether they were important and sufficient.

Wednesday, the 16th of February. This morning Carl Sigismund Ott was married to the maiden Anna Magdalena Heinrich. Her brothers and sisters, with the exception of a sixteen year old brother, are all at our place, and are very well looked after, and they also give us good hope that they will cause themselves to be grounded further and further in the good that they have begun. This woman and her brother were sold into service in Augusta more than four years ago by Captain Thomson.[12] But, because the trader who bought them acted very barbarous and heathenish towards them and because complaints were made to the authorities about it, they were taken to Savannah where the woman served out her time and her brother has still to serve until his twenty-fifth year.[13] She, like other young women, was in great peril in Savannah of seduction and also had opportunity to marry ill-bred people; but the love for her brothers and sisters drew her here, and I hope that it will redound not only to her physical but also her spiritual and eternal profit.

Thursday, the 17th of February. A man remembered in his last, painful illness that in his youth he had harmed the property of his parents and other people; and he promised then, at the penitent recognition of his sins, to make restitution in money or money equivalent. This he did just today in such a way as he could not have imagined on his very sick-bed, for what he donated redounded at our public divine services especially to the honor of Jesus Christ and to the service of His members.

Monday, the 21st of February. Today the people from the plantations began to split rails for our orphanage.[14] They are for fencing in a large field near the city towards the Savannah River, so that Kalcher can graze the horses there winter and summer and can thus be saved from the far-flung and troublesome

search for them whenever we have need of one for the perfo-
mance of our office, which must happen quite often. A good
quantity of hay will be made here and will be carried home easily
because the area is near and people can easily get there with
wagons and horses. A district was cleared already seven years
ago of trees and bushes; but it is mostly forest of every kind
where there is grass, both winter and summer. If we have
enough means, a field can be prepard for cultivating local crops.
The congregation will gladly grant that to the orphanage because no one is harmed by it, rather the profit from it extends to
the congregation. Each and every household from the plantations works only two days gratis at this communal labor: and the
fence will be built in such a way that it requires yearly only a little
repair without much trouble and expense. Just this year they
have taken to such fencemaking which by and by everyone will
pursue because the labor is not much greater and is of much
greater durability. The fence will also be built up over six feet
high so that none of the horses can jump over it. It is also so
strong that no wind can knock it down. We cannot build similar
rail-fences in the city because the poultry can creep through or
fly over, hence we make them from six-foot long planks.

Tuesday, the 22nd of February. Today on the plantations as
well as here in town in the evening prayer hours I finished
(praise God!) the 23rd chapter of I Chronicles; and with the assistance of the Holy Spirit we had right much blessing and edification, for which may our faithful God be praised. We learned
today from the above-mentioned story and its latter part that
David called upon his servants with moving and impressive
words to aid his son Solomon in the building of the temple.
Without a doubt a fine prefiguration lies in this and also this
lesson, that it is not only a duty for the faithful but also a great
honor, in the construction of the spiritual temple in the New
Testament, to be assistants to the Lord Jesus as to the real Solomon would apply not only to righteous ministers but also
Christian fathers and mothers of households.[15] It is without
doubt God's purpose also to build amongst us His spiritual temple from pure, living stones of born-again souls, as He has already made a beginning in grace. In addition to the great
strengthening of my faith I recognize, amongst other things,

from the following circumstances that occurred almost at the same time that He wished to progress in this most important and blessed work: 1) The church on the plantations is now constructed to the point that we will soon be able to hold divine services in it, and no one has been harmed in the least in accomplishing it and all workers have worked with great courage and in right Christian harmony. 2) Although the heads of households on the plantations have a great deal to do in their households and in their farming on account of the approach of spring, they nonetheless went with willingness and great diligence to the labor on the important fencebuilding which was mentioned yesterday, whose goal was to advance the divine services on the plantations and the business of our offices.

3) We apply the word of David that we observed today, or rather the words of God through him, fairly in faith to ourselves, viz., I Chronicles: 23, "Is not the Lord your God with you? And hath he not given you rest on every side?" For the kindness and omnipotence of God is, therefore, all the more to be marveled at, that we even so enjoy noble peace and rest, also complete freedom of conscience although there is war and unrest everywhere and our country lies just on the border. He is doing that certainly for the reason that He also wishes to build amongst us a spiritual house and sanctuary. 4) We can tell from the letters we have received that the Lord has again awakened his servants, our Fathers and benefactors, to labor on the construction of the spiritual temple at Ebenezer by means of encouragement and generous gifts of money, books, and medications; and they are now doing it right faithfully. David contributed his wherewithal in gold, silver, and other materials to the construction of the temple during his sadness and at a troublesome time, as it says in I Chronicles 23:14 according to the basic text. Although this applies chiefly to our Savior, who in his condition of humility merited for us all the abundance of God's grace, nonetheless this circumstance impresses us in view of the gifts we have received.[16]

We are also impressed that in Germany at this troublesome time of war they indeed flowed together (as we see from the specifications) from some people in their poverty. Their faithful and zealous prayer for Ebenezer and heartfelt wishes for blessings that have been showered down upon us in the letters and elsewhere, we consider to be a very great treasure. They belong with our current text of faith: "We have a firm city, its walls are whole."

It pleases us greatly that none of the letters from our Fathers and friends written to us poor ones in this perilous time of war have been lost so far since so many ships are being captured. We take it to be a sign of God's grace over us and rouse ourselves fairly to apply well, amidst heartfelt prayer, the awakenings and comforts written to us, given by God Himself and preserved and brought here in defiance of the enemy. May He cause all words to go to our hearts, or they have flowed to us from faithful hearts.

Wednesday, the 23rd of February. Oh! How it has gladdened us to find in the letters we have received new assurance from the fervent intercession of the faithful in Europe for our Ebenezer. In those perilous times of war, especially in the fearsome attack of the Spanish on this colony, our dear Lord has caused us to enjoy this assurance right abundantly, to the strengthening of our faith and of those in Europe. Indeed, to the edification of myself, and I hope others, I can do nothing other than put here a point from the letter of the dear Mr. N., whose intercession and whose friends' powerful intercession for us is relevant:

> The fall that our dear brother Gronau had from his horse alarmed me and others. Since the letter came just at the hour when I and several close friends wished to pray, we took it much to heart and laid it before Jesus, crying: 'Jesus, dear master! Take pity on our Gronau, etc.', and thus we did quite simply with you, with Mr. Vigera, Mr. Meyer, and so on until we had prayed through all of Ebenezer. May the Lord grant our wish and proceed to strengthen them, to the praise of His magnificent grace, to the wellbeing of their dear family, to the edification of the entire congregation, and also to ourselves, especially of the comfort and refreshment of my friends.

Thursday, the 24th of February. Because my dear colleague Boltzius has traveled to Savannah, I am now holding the prayer hours, and I am repeating in them that piece of the story of the passion which we contemplated last Sunday, for it is necessary that we diligently ponder the same. Not in vain did the Lord

Jesus tell the three disciples who were to witness His last mortal struggle that they should keep watch and pray. Ah! How necessary it is nonetheless for us to encourage each other so that we might indeed apply the present time well! The Passion of Christ has a special strength, as many amongst us experience. Now, whenever I come to my parishioners, I like speaking with them of it, and it is my desire to become so familiar with Christ Crucified that I know nothing else but Him. May the Lord teach me to keep watch and pray! Amongst other things when we considered the story of the passion the little verse from Zacharia 13:7 was very sweet for us, as it says: "I will turn mine hand upon the little ones." Ah! Who will harm us then? And what then shall we lack? God's hand is full of blessings.

Friday, the 25th of February. We (especially myself, Boltzius) might have met with a great misfortune on our trip down, as I sat at the helm; for in the moonlight our boat struck with the greatest violence one of the trees hanging from the shore into the water. It might have almost ripped the boat around and thrown me out or injured me by means of a perilous jolt, if God were not the aid and protection of myself and all of us. We thought upon the gospel from last Sunday and what was read aloud to us from it from Hebrews 1:14: "Are they not all ministering spirits, sent forth," etc., also: "He shall give his angels charge concerning thee, and in their hands . . . " etc. Our dear Lord must sometimes cause one to come into distress and peril so that one may learn to recognize and praise one's own nothingness and on the other hand the protecting and helping kindness of God.

A merchant in Savannah received a large amount of used men's clothing from London and sold it very cheaply. A piece of clothing that otherwise might cost 4 pounds Sterling is being given away here for around 16 shillings and less and even so seems little worn. That would be a trade for our inhabitants, to whom I have given news thereof upon my return today. In times of peace, clothes like these are said to be sold off to Spain; they garnish them with their gold and silver laces or trimmings and put on airs with them. Because there is now no trade with them, people in England don't know what to do with them; and here they can be brought to the people right well, especially since clothing is very costly.

MARCH

Tuesday, the 1st of March. It was very impressive for us to see from the fatherly writings of Senior Urlsperger that our dear Lord collected all kinds of loving gifts for Ebenezer from the month of March to the end of August, and therefore during the time that the Spaniards intended to destroy everything in Georgia. If God gathers, His enemies cannot scatter, which perceptibly strengthens our faith in this perilous time of war. When I told the schoolchildren near town about the pious daughter of a pious mother in A. and other lambs of the Lord Jesus, who in love and simplicity contributed what they had for Ebenezer[1], I also made it known to the children and adults here. When I told them that the former was now already a maiden of the Lamb in the Church Triumphant and had the little verse read aloud: "They are virgins and follow the Lamb," etc., a stream of tears broke out in the eyes of a little girl, as it were, which increased and strengthened the emotion which I and others had already felt.

Wednesday, the 2nd of March. During the trip I was told that twenty-four long boards belonging to Theobald Kieffer, which he and Hans Flerl very painstakingly cut some time ago on his plantation, caught fire and were completely burned. Only a couple were saved by a man who had come there. He had indeed, as a precaution, burned away the grass thereabouts, but the day before yesterday the wind grew very strong and likely drove some burning chips onto the boards. The site where the boards lay is rather far from his house and field; and, besides that, he traveled to Savannah on Monday, so that his family were little aware of the accident. So far our dear Lord has turned the greatest and biggest harm away from us in grace and only now and again inflicted a small misfortune or chastisement so that we are reminded gratefully to recognize His great kindness upon us and to humble ourselves before Him on account of our sins, also more diligently to preserve what is ours with a faithful prayer.[2]

Thursday, the 3rd of March. This afternoon, together with three intelligent men, I took the trouble to investigate and resolve some matters of contention, at which God caused us to sense His blessing. Some people have quite often abused our kindness and heeded good admonitions but little, hence it has been necessary to be very serious with them, nonetheless to be so in an orderly manner for the improvement of themselves and others.

Saturday, the 5th of March. What an impresssion of the paternal care of God must have made on the Salzburg family that has its work and provisioning in the orphanage as long as God wishes, when I read aloud to them and everyone else what had been written in July of the past year: "When some friends in V. heard that a Salzburg family had reached Court Chaplain Ziegenhagen in London and were to be dispatched to Ebenezer, the friends directed 11 gulden for the purpose."[3]

From this they could recognize that they had come to Ebenezer according to God's will and under His special loving care: if now the parents and their three children will fear, love, and trust this faithful God above all else, He will care for them further if they wish to start up their own plantation and household.[4]

Sunday, the 6th of March. Last night Mrs. Sanftleben gave birth to two children, to wit, a little son and little daughter; and, because the latter was weakly, I was called to his plantation on Ebenezer Creek after 1 p.m. to baptize her, which duly took place. I would have baptized the little boy; but the father and the midwife, Mrs. Rheinländer, were of the opinion that he was strong enough to be brought to church and baptized publicly. Before the morning divine services had been started I got the news that the little boy, who was said to be the stronger, had died, just as the father had gone out to appoint the godparents, and neither Mrs. Rheinländer nor anyone else of those present had administered emergency baptism. I found this no other way but extremely distasteful. We know from God's word that Christian children who die without holy baptism are not cursed for that reason because we, to be sure, but not the Lord God, are bound to the means of grace. Nonetheless a heavy responsibility falls on those who do nothing or who do the wrong thing in the matter. The parents feel pure distress and unrest, especially as they have been taught from God's word what a great treasure holy baptism is and what an honor it is for our children to receive even in their childhood that which Christ our Lord and head received upon taking up His ministry in the Jordan, Matthew 3:13 ff.

As I was reading through the very pleasant letter from Professor Francke, I thought of what happened to me right after the prayer in the edification hour, to wit, someone sent me a fine cane to use when traveling out to the plantations. Thereupon I thought of the little verse Sirach 2:3 "Cling to him, forsake him not; thus will your future be great," etc., which once an old disciple of Christ in Halle gave to me upon the commencement of the journey I took for my health mostly on foot. He requested that I remember it each time that I took a staff in my hand to take a journey. God is also great in small things, wherein skepticism laughs, to be sure: yet faith still finds good substance. For it comes to pass with our dear Lord and in His kingdom and amongst His children quite simply but also very wisely; proud reason knows nothing of that.

Monday, the 7th of March. Today we celebrated our annual memorial and thanksgiving feast, and simultaneously we dedicated the lovely new church with prayer and God's word, for which our dear Lord presented us with weather we wished for: dry, quiet, and temperate. Everyone in turn, large and small, who could get away at all traveled to the celebration of this feast, which is so joyful to us; and, because both parents and children were on the plantations together, the gathering in the church grew as numerous as we had hardly ever seen. After 8 o'clock the divine services commenced, when the entire congregation, standing before the countenance of the Lord, gave voice to the hymn *Komm, Heiliger Geist, Herre Gott,* etc.; and after that the important 16th chapter of 2 Chronicles was read aloud, then two songs of praise were sung and, instead of reading the epistle aloud as usual, the children recited the 26th chapter of Isaiah, indeed several times, by means of which it became more familiar to the congregation.

In the afternoon the children recited the 115th Psalm, between the first and second hymns, and at the commencement of the divine services the 20th chapter of 2 Chronicles was read aloud, in which, just as in chapter 16, material is present that is very edifying and pertinent to the circumstances of our feast.

The morning text was taken from the 115th Psalm, vv. 17–18: "The dead praise not the Lord, neither any that go down into silence. But we will bless the Lord from this time forth and for evermore. Praise the Lord." Our miraculous God has still kept us in life and in the priceless time of grace, on the other hand since the last memorial and thanksgiving festival quite many adults and children have been called from us into eternity through temporal death. We looked upon this important circumstance particularly with this text. The introductory words were from Isaiah 26:12, "Lord, thou wilt ordain peace for us: for thou also hast wrought all our works in us." From it we perceived 1) that true Christians are not lazy people and slothful but rather fulfillers of the will of God, compare Acts 13:36 and Matthew 25:23. 2) that whenever in their general and particular callings they make progress and accomplish something they ascribe it not to their strength and ability but rather to the Lord, and they give Him all honor.

Since it is now impossible to deny and it is even apparent to strangers that much has been accomplished in Ebenezer in quite many ways, we must also call out today: "Ebenezer, the Lord has helped us to here! For that praise and glory are due Him from now and for evermore."[5] Just as the divine services began with prayer on bended knee after the hymn *Komm, Heiliger Geist,* etc., so we knelt down once more after the sermon had closed and implored God in the name of Christ for a contrite and faithful heart and in this state for forgiveness of sins. Thereupon we praised Him for all His spiritual and physical benefactions and prayed for our worthy benefactors by name.

In the afternoon my dear colleague had as text Isaiah 26:1–4. At that time people would sing such a hymn in the country of Judah: *Wir haben eine feste Stadt,* etc. The introductory words were: "The name of the Lord is a strong tower," (Proverbs 18:10) and the gospel was expounded to the congregation for the first time in this church in such a way that, if they had caused their hearts to incline to obedience, even today they might have been able to become the most blessed people. We do not doubt that this imperishable seed will also have found hearts within which it will take root by itself and will bring forth its fruit above itself.

Tuesday, the 8th of March. Amongst the physical benefactions our dear Lord has manifested in these days to us two and to the orphanage, we rightly count the great, stout fence that the men of the plantations have built around a large piece of land containing more than 400 acres near town on the Savannah River. It was completely finished today; and in it will be put to pasture the horses of the orphanage and ourselves, which we need because of our office. More than four thousand rails, each 13 foot long, were split. On the one side the Savannah River serves instead of the fence and in the direction of the bridge the new fence butts against the one that some men finished communally around their land this spring and is of the same durability. Who knows what our dear Lord has in mind, for this great field in time can be used for something better than mere pasture and hay making. Praise God! In this great forest, close by the town, lies the land that the first and third transports planted in the first years. It has now lain fallow and rested for four years; because the great roots have rotted, by and by we will be able to use the plow on it.

Friday, the 11th of March. Today in the second edification hour in the new church our dear Lord caused us one joy after the other and at the same time drew tears from the hearts and eyes of many parishioners. I wish shortly to explain the reason for it. We sang the beautiful hymn: *Es kostet viel ein Christ zu seyn,* etc. After I had prayed briefly about it and called to our dear Lord for His blessing on our holy purpose, I reminded them that 1) I would like for some of the parishioners from the plantations whom God has given good voices and who have the gift of song to come together at a certain hour to learn the unfamiliar old and new songs as was done in the city so that amongst us in song as in other items things might go harmoniously and refreshingly. We would be happy to serve them therein according to our ability. I would like them to learn first the song that was learned in town: *Zion, du heilige Gottes-Stadt,* etc. In that way they might acquire the ability to be able to sing it publicly in the church with us. For the song would have to be so dear to us because the new church received from God's miraculous and gracious dispensation the edifying name Zion Church, just as the one in town was called Jerusalem Church. I recounted herewith that our abundantly loving God had arranged things as miraculously with the naming of these churches as He had done with the naming of the town we were planning: Ebenezer.

When some young Salzburgers of the first transport traveled with Mr. Oglethorpe, the surveyors, and some Englishmen to the place we were to settle, I wrote letters in Savannah to Europe; in Savannah I learned from an Englishman who had just returned that the city we were planning was to be called Ebenezer. I rejoiced at that right heartily, especially as I noted that the Lord had His hand in the matter and it was neither the counsel nor the fancy of men. Mr. Oglethorpe was so pleased by the name that soon thereafter he mentioned it with pleasure in a letter to London. Thus our faithful Lord, whom it pleases to edify us in every way, has once more arranged things so that, contrary to our thought and intention, our two churches received the abovementioned names, which without doubt will bring more edification than if they had been named for dead saints or even for a papist spiritual order.

Mr. Muhlenberg had asked me what the name of our town church was; I did not know what to say to him at the time; but, after the prayer hour last Tuesday evening, when I wrote something in the diary and the important benefactions that our dear Lord manifested to our congregation already at the beginning of this year had gone to my heart, the names Zion and Jerusalem occured to me while I was writing, as names for the two churches; my heart grew full of joy and amazement at the divine kindness. Whenever I wrote letters to our Fathers and benefactors, these names were right sweet to me, and I have been assured that our churches have received them according to God's loving counsel.

Today, prior to the edification hour the authoritative gospel verse (Zachariah 9:9) occurred to me: "Rejoice greatly, O daughter of Zion; shout, O daughter of Jerusalem; behold, thy King cometh unto thee: he is just and having salvation." These words (Third Sunday after Epiphany) were especially blessed for us in the sermon; and, because the new church was being built at that time, we wished that this magnificent authoritative verse, in which Christ with His kingdom, subjects, magnificent privileges, and benefactions stand together, might be written above its doorway. And behold, now God has arranged that both churches and our parishioners who belong to both churches are included in this verse; and at the same time they are addressed in the most kindly manner: "Rejoice greatly, O daughter of Zion; shout, O daughter of Jerusalem," etc. 2) I explained to them the first part of the contents of the letter from General Oglethorpe, and it was indeed right impressive to us when he wrote: "I depend upon just that God who has protected us always," etc. The name Ebenezer was here once again very edifying to us. 3) I repeated in the last quarter hour the recently recited points about 2 Peter 1:1, and today added the second very important and right valuable verse. How strengthened we were when we all departed!

Saturday, the 12th of March. Our dear Lord has arranged for the young Lackner girl on the plantations willingly to present a stout sheet of twill for use in the Zion church, although she is poor herself; and today Mrs. /Elisabeth/ Meyer, who is still laboring with the illness she had in Germany, sent one just like it for use in the daily prayer hours in the Jerusalem church. May the God of blessings reward both dear persons and their families for the gift. For on Sundays we are already provided with soft table cloths which, however, we save whenever possible because they cost much, and therefore the ones now sent to us for use during the week are very dear to us.

Just as I was writing these lines the honest Austrian Schmidt called on me and recounted how in yesterday's prayer hour our dear Lord gave him and his wife many edifying impressions and gave both of them this resolution to present something to the church. Before he could say a word at home, he explained, his wife indicated just that linen cloth for a table cover that he had in mind to present to the church. He said God had granted him very many good things both spiritual and physical so far and in the summer had granted him a little legacy, and with it the same above mentioned cloth; he said he would gladly turn over the cloth to us if we wished to accept it. I showed him what Mrs. Meyer had presented to us and told him that his good will was as dear to our dear Lord as the deed, and I thanked him for his love. And so he kept the cloth but in its place presented some shillings to the church.

Sunday, the 13th of March. In today's prayer hour I remembered what Steiner had recounted to me at the memorial and thanksgiving celebration, to wit, that he and others had had a good deal of profit at the time of the Spanish invasion. He explained that they had to stand guard in shifts on the plantations as they had done in town. When they wished to begin the guard each evening they all got down on their knees together and prayed right zealously to the Father in the name of Christ, whereupon they mutually received great joy, and stood watch and patrolled joyfully throughout the night.

Wednesday, the 16th of March. Mr. Thomas Jones received me (Boltzius), who had traveled to Savannah, with very kind affection. Without my asking again he then paid me the great benefaction in money that the Lord Trustees had ordered for the inhabitants of this country and also our people in 1739.[6] This inspired me and others to great praise of God because He was now doing anew to us just what we had perceived last Sunday from the Gospel according to John 6:1 and the little passage at 1 Timothy 6:17. We should put our hope in the living God who bestows upon us abundantly all kinds of things for our enjoyment. In His wisdom and kindness in the previous week from our memorial and thanksgiving celebration onwards, He has granted us quite magnificent opportunities to aspire to the kingdom of God and His rigtheousness: and He therefore causes the physical things to devolve upon us which fairly strengthen us in our faith and remind us of our Evangelical duty to be obedient and thankful to Him.

I, and others with me, believe that the benefaction, which came to 174 pounds Sterling, would not have been as pleasing and impressive if we had gotten it in the previous time, as we did others, when He finally presented it to us after long practice of our faith and waiting, during which the thoughts in the hearts of many became clear, when He built for Himself amongst us a Zion and Jerusalem and caused a few serious reports of the intended new attack of the Spanish to reach our ears. The beautiful text of Psalms 132, vv. 13–16 has to be fairly comforting to us in these circumstances: "For the Lord hath chosen Zion; he hath desired it for his habitation. This is my rest forever: here will I dwell; for I have desired it. I will abundantly bless her provision:

I will satisfy her poor with bread. I will also clothe her priests with salvation: and her saints shall shout aloud for joy."

Mr. Jones recounted to me amongst other things an old story not unknown to the English, to wit, that once after the English had triumphed over France but afterwards had suffered great loss therefrom, a French officer sneeringly asked an Englishman whether and when they would come again to France and do themselves harm, and the latter (the English officer) answered: indeed, to be sure, when your sins cry more loudly and strongly to heaven than ours. Mr. Jones compared the story to the current state of affairs. At that, to our mutual joy, the momentous words of God occured to me: Isaiah 65:8, "Thus saith the Lord. As the new wine is found in the cluster, and one saith, Destroy it not; for a blessing is in it: so will I do for my servants' sakes, that I may not destroy them all."

Thursday, the 17th of March. This morning my dear colleague and I were busy distributing the so-called bounty amongst our parishioners who had a harvest in 1739, to which end they had gathered from the plantations at my chambers. We had previously calculated this great present from the Lord Trustees in German money, and it amounted to more than a thousand five hundred royal gulden. Certainly a benefaction for which we have great cause to glorify the Lord and to pray for the worthy Lord Trustees, most especially for General Oglethorpe, from whose foresight the current payment of the bounty was flowing, since Col. Stephens was out of money. I first suggested to the men gathered there, and requested at the same time, that they might consider whether or not the long delay of this promised benefaction might have opened one and another unfaithful, mistrustful, bad tempered, and censorious hearts. I said they had cause to humble themselves penitently before the Lord and to seek forgiveness for the sake of Christ. I am often astounded at the great things that God has done in Ebenezer, already this year too; and, before I am aware of it, God does new miracles of His kindness amongst us and to us, and we are also struck by what we learned recently at the memorial and thanksgiving celebration, from Isaiah 26:15: "O Lord, thou hast increased the nation: thou art glorified: thou hast removed it far unto all the ends of the earth."

A pious Salzburger reminded me of the verse we had for a text in 1739 on our day of thanksgiving for the harvest we received; it had been dedicated to us from Augsburg at that time of war, Joel 2:21: "Fear not, O land: for the Lord will do great things."[7] It cannot possibly be by chance that I received the letter in which the Lord Trustees promised us the bounty which we distributed today, just at our last day of thanksgiving for the harvest we received. Now our dear Lord causes it to be paid us in cash, when we have hardly celebrated our annual memorial and thanksgiving festival and dedicated our Church of Zion. And all this is happening at the time when we hear much of war and the rumors of war. May God cause our faith to be strengthened thereby, and may He also give our parishioners the grace to receive this benefaction with gratitude, and may it be blessed by God's word and prayer.

After the distribution we praised God together, and during this blessed exercise I was especially impressed by the verse that I had read this morning with my family, Psalm 145, vv. 15–16: "The eyes of all wait upon thee, etc., Thou openest thine hand, and satisfiest, etc." For the heavenly Father has indeed opened over us His hand that is full of blessings. Hence at a time of war we enjoy the noble peace and otherwise many spiritual and physical benefactions.

Friday, the 18th of March. Mr. Vigera came no further this time than Port Royal, although he had already traveled away before our memorial and thanksgiving festival with the intent of seeing Charleston and taking care of some errands there. He inspected some plantations in the vicinity of Port Royal and cannot find words to describe the bad, evilly organized way of life of the whites and Negroes. He communicated to me the letter written to him by the worthy Mr. N. of the 5th November of last year. It impressed me greatly. This dear benefactor not only did a great favor at our small beginning of wine and silk growing but also made all kinds of very good suggestions about the most advantageous way to plant mulberry trees, to spin the silk, etc. He refers to a certain little silkmaking booklet that is said to have been sent to us but has still not arrived. I am hoping that Mr. Vigera will answer this fine letter in detail.

There was progress this year in sericulture and also in the or-

phanage. I only regret that we did not have the proper opportunity to accommodate the silk worms. One should have a spe-
cific house for it. For in the house where there are foodstocks,
ants and midges easily get in and they kill the worms and thereafter soon infect the healthy worms so that they turn yellow and
quickly die off. We also need boards for separating them properly from one another and cleaning them often because filth and
stench are harmful to them. Because the planting and cultivation of the fields are proceeding just when the worms come out
and the mulberry trees bear leaves, the people will be unable at
this time properly to attend to the sericulture. If they could just
cultivate more German crops and do without the local crops of
this country, they would have more time, for then the fields
would already be cultivated in fall and winter.[8] But with God's
blessing one thing will follow another, and we have to stay with
the small thing until we are led into the greater.

Saturday, the 19th of March. This morning in Thomas
Bacher's dwelling our gracious God sent me a very pleasurable
short hour. The parents and their two daughters came into the
house from the fields, and I became involved in an intimate conversation with them about some practical truths of Christianity;
therein we felt the gracious presence of God to our mutual
awakening, so that I believe they will not so soon forget its in-
dications. The older girl wishes seriously to become a bride of
the Lamb and to prepare herself in this order for confirmation
and the first taking of Holy Communion. Perhaps the Lord will
bless her example in her sister, who is now, to be sure, obliging
but still frivolous.

Monday, the 21st of March. This morning we consecrated Simon Reiter's house with the word of God and with prayer.
Various people from the neighborhood had gathered for it. The
husband told me that yesterday he had called upon our dear
Lord Himself to give me what I had to read from holy scripture
for the dedication of the house, with him and others. After the
hour was over he recounted to me with joy and praise of God
that he had been abundantly edified by the divine truths that I
had read aloud. He said he believed that God had intended this
especially for himself and his family. It was the first two verses
from 2 Peter 1. First there were prayer and supplications to the

God of all grace for that which is especially necessary for ourselves and our benefactors, and all this in the name of our Lord Jesus Christ.

Wednesday, the 23rd of March. Kornberger has constructed a new dwelling that was consecrated in a Christian manner today. Because the first chapter from 2 Peter became so dear to us and because God has created in our souls till now so much profit through it I have resolved, with God, to read something aloud from it from now on at house consecrations. The material that is present in them is especially well suited to such Christian activity. Our kind Lord Himself has led my spirit to it and so I am promising myself with the assistance of His spirit many further blessings from it.

Saturday, the 26th of March. The provision allowance for those people at our place who were servants to the Lord Trustees was sent to me from Savannah.[9] It was reported therewith that the President and his committe members[10] had appropriated 14 Pounds that is to be paid them very soon instead of the brood swine and poultry.

Tuesday, the 29th of March. N's young wife has been unattentive and frivolous for some time, thereby causing her husband and us concern as well as giving offence to other people. But for some weeks the word of the Lord has been able to penetrate her so that she is coming to a recognition of her misery[11] and of divine sadness; today she made an acknowledgement of it to me. Her mother, the otherwise righteous N., clung to this daugher with an all too great, improper, and consequently harmful love and harmed not only this daughter but also her own soul. She was also under the delusion, as is often wont to happen in such a case, that people were doing too much to her. This N. is one of our first school children, on whom we worked faithfully, by God's grace, in the school and in the church; and till now it has always occurred with hope. If the seed that has been broadcast finally sprouts and brings forth fruits of penitence, faith, and piety, then the joy amongst the spiritual laborers is very great and encourages them further in the hope of working on even the worst of persons in the greatest possible fidelity and of despairing of no one.

Thursday, the 31st of March. When I rode in this afternoon

from the plantations, a woman coming from the mill told me
that during church service this morning N. suffered great harm
because of a conflagration which very quickly burned down his
kitchen and hut. I could not learn for certain whether or not his
furniture was saved. God without doubt wishes to awaken this
man and his wife from their sleep of sin and death, in which till
now they have continued to sleep, much powerful compassion of
the Holy Spirit notwithstanding. May He nonetheless wish that
it be a blessing, according to His mercy, so that they not only
wake up but also arise by means of true conversion.

APRIL

Friday, the 1st of April. Today, Good Friday, the high Day of
Atonement of the New Testament, our gracious Lord once more
showed us many good things. Not only did He refresh our arid
earth with a right penetrating rain during the afternoon church
service but also by means of the preaching of the gospel of the
death and burial of Christ as also by means of the enjoyment of
Holy Communion. He caused pure grace to rain down upon us,
so that the hearts of the penitent and faithful amongst us were
moistened and refreshed right bountifully with the blood of reconciliation of Christ, to their vindication, salvation, and
glorification. Ninety-three of us went to the Lord's table, to
which till now He invited us by means of the word of His passion
in the most kindly manner.

This too contributed to our greater edification: that today
four young girls, who till now have received the milk of the gospel in the preparation hours for the recognition and practice of
piety, renewed their baptismal vows before God and His congregation. At the same time they were confirmed, consecrated,
and thereupon allowed for the first time to the Lord's table. Yesterday instead of our morning sermon we examined them on
the words of Acts 13:26, " . . . to you is the word of this salvation
sent," etc., which, praise God! brought them and others much
edification. Today they vowed with hand and mouth to become
and to remain wise virgins and to follow after the Lamb wherever it goes.

Saturday, the 2nd of April. I learned while visiting at a house that some people of the 4th transport are suffering great difficulty because they lack cows, and hence milk. They would consider it a great benefaction if they could get even sour milk from which the cream has been skimmed. This caused me to compose a written petition to the authorities in Savannah and to explain to them therein that the 4th transport has had provision allowance for only six months; and, although our old inhabitants have done their utmost for them, nonetheless such assistance does not extend far enough that they can have their necessary support from their share until the harvest.

Now, because milk is a great help in the households of poor people and because the Lord Trustees most graciously promised cows and other livestock for this 4th transport in a letter to me, and also because now is the best time to make cows tame and manageable, I am asking that the President and his assistants take the need of these people to heart and at least furnish the poorest with a few cows. By that they will be, doubtless, acting according to the wish of General Oglethorpe and the Lord Trustees. If, however, they are unable to come to this resolution, I am asking that they furnish me with six cows and calves from the Lord Trustees' livestock in Old Ebenezer, for the poorest, for which I am promising to pay, in case the Lord Trustees alter their wish and do not desire to give the cows that were promised.

For preparation for the holy celebration that God once more has caused us to live to see in good health and good peace, we examined last week on the third day of Easter the important epistle Acts 13:26; and we received much material for edification from it. I learned that our gracious Lord blessed greatly the evening prayer hours for N. so that he is establishing a right firm foundation in his Christianity. Therefore, God in His great mercy is substituting in spiritual things what is missing for him in physical care of the body and refreshment, since his wife is still constantly ill.

Tuesday, the 5th of April. Some time ago I had inquired of Mrs./Margaretha/ Lackner of the 3rd transport whether she, too, was seeking with heartfelt prayer to impress the gospel verses that she heard in the sermons into her memory and mind. This has served her well till now, so that she is more diligent in learning than otherwise; and today, when I visited, she knew

how to say various edifying verses from the 115th Psalm. I
showed both husband and wife that amidst their labor they
ought to consider calmly not only the words but also what was
placed in their hearts from them in the sermons and to experience the power of the divine truth. Yesterday the gospel of the
celebration, Luke 24:13 ff., gave us the opportunity to profit
from the content of the important words at Ephesians 4:29: "Let
no corrupt communication proceed out of your mouth, but that
which is good to the use of edifying, that it may minister grace
unto the hearers." God presented us with much edification from
it; and today I learned that it had given the listeners a great impression, especially as they had received instructions on how to
carry on a pious conversation also on their way to church, like
the *Emahuntische Jünger*,[1] and continue it at home, which will not
remain without blessing.

Two men from the plantations at the Ebenezer Creek were at
my house and asked that God's word might be preached for
them, too, a few times weekly as was done in the Zion Church on
the plantations. Their plantations lie near to town, to be sure;
but, because we hold the prayer hours in the evening when they
are tired from work and besides have things to do with their livestock, especially since they still have no herdsman, it is greatly
inconvenient for them constantly to attend the prayer hours in
the Jerusalem Church; and therefore we probably will have to
accede to their request. May God grant us the time, strength,
and fitness for this important matter!

Wednesday, the 6th of April. In our emerging town so many
expenses are required during the first arrangements that other
people could hardly imagine them. Although our inhabitants
have their physical support by means of God's blessing, they are
nonetheless not in a position to contribute something to one or
another necessary arrangement, e.g. construction of the church,
support of the orphanage or the mill, etc. Hence we see it fairly
as a very great benefaction of God that some benefactors in Europe are still always inclined and willing to contribute something in physical gifts for the benefit of our little Ebenezer. May
our omniscient God and merciful Father abundantly recom-
pense them and their children both here and there for it. There
are also needy persons amongst us who, on account of illness

and other incidents with their house and farming arrangements, need essential assistance, similar ones are amongst the
last transport who have only received a half-years's provision allowance, since the Lord Trustees were not able to accomplish
anything more.

Friday, the 8th of April. An old man from Purysburg /Krüsy/
worked for some time for daily wages at our place; and, since he
has been in Purysburg for a few days, he is now already returning and declaring that he would do it for the sake of serving God
and that he desires nothing else but to prepare himself for eternity. He has become so fond of our place that he is quite desirous
of moving here. He told me that while in Purysburg he had lost
his hearing as he slept; by and by, he said, he could hear just a
little in one ear; but God listened with grace to his sighs and the
common prayer for him, and once more gave him his sound
hearing when he had been with us a short while.

Saturday, the 9th of April. The fields of wheat, corn, barley,
and oats give very good hay after this harvest, which with these
crops is in the middle of summer. It is indeed the wish of myself
and others that more fields would be sown with similar European seeds. This year rather more has been planted than in the
previous years, nonetheless no one else has engaged in plowing
except the orphanage.

Monday, the 11th of April. This morning I visited both heads
of household, Zant and Glaner, who have their plantations next
to one another between the town and the Mill River. They are
still dwelling in one hut together because the brief time and
their previous bodily weakness have not allowed either of them
to build his own hut, kitchen, and stalls. I was greatly pleased to
hear that these married couples were living together in right
Christian unity and service and were edifying themselves by
prayer and the word of God. Because this morning I read with
new good purpose the short instruction on how one is to read
holy scripture for one's true edification, I showed them just that
in their little Canstein Bible,[2] and told them how they could advance their private edification according to the directions of
these few pages.

Wednesday, the 13th of April. Some quite small school children are still certainly standing in the grace of baptism; may the

true Shepherd keep them, and may He seek the others who have strayed from Him until He finds them and has taken them upon His shoulders so that they might know how good a resting place it is. Now may the Lord Jesus be humbly praised for all assistance, and may He make me His proper shepherd's helper, for whom the doorkeeper opens so that all those who do not wantonly struggle against it might be brought to Jesus, the proper High Shepherd and also the Doorway for the sheep, so that they may have life and full sufficiency with Him.

I traveled out to the plantations on Ebenezer Creek and made arrangements with the men there for holding the edification hour at their place. Afterwards I spoke with some families especially and heard how things stood with them regarding their Christianity. One man told me how edifying the sermon for Easter and last Sunday was. He said that his mortal enemy,[3] however, was keeping him so busy that often he did not know what he should do; he said also that his physical strength ebbed because of it. But he recognizes quite well what our dear Lord is seeking thereby, to wit, to humble him properly so that he will not make too much of himself, for he knows well how otherwise he has liked to set himself above others.[4]

With the other family, who just moved to our place, I spoke while they were working. When the husband opined that, when he was working he had God in his heart, I asked him if he knew it for certain and whence he knew it. When the answer was badly composed and had shallow reasoning, I showed that God does not dwell naturally in man, rather the devil has his effects in him. I said that this must first be extirpated, then God could enter therein with His grace. I said the man must first seek to experience it in this order, otherwise it was nothing.

Thursday, the 14th of April. Our butcher was with me in Savannah and has made the business with certain cows and oxen very certain. Thereby the care of God, to his own and to the orphanage's favor, became quite beautifully and distinctly clear; and the business has now been so arranged and prescribed that we need worry no further about any inconvenience or unrest. In like manner the owner also profited from this transaction greatly, for he would have lost track of many cattle because of an unfaithful man in the country if our own people had not intervened. Most people in this country play games with oaths, and whoever can pull the wool best over the next man's eyes will become rich after a while. Upon my lodging the request, the authorties promised to give to the poorest of the 4th transport six cows and six calves from their herd in Old Ebenezer until the Lord Trustees certify it and allow the remainder to have some cattle. Also the Lord Trustees once more have proven themselves very kind to me regarding my advice and have taken my suggestion in some things.

Friday, the 15th of April. In my house I have had several hundred silk worms that have dimished in number every night. When we paid attention closely at night, we found on the silk worms a large number of great brown beetles, of which in the houses of this country there are uncommonly many. By and by the beetles destroyed them.

Saturday, the 16th of April. A righteous man told me that at the Easter festival God sent such great blessings from His word into his heart as he had never had in previous times. He said, however, that at last Sunday's exposition of the eighth commandment he grew quite downcast, since his old sins against this commandment, which consist specifically of the theft of some fruit, were awakened anew in his conscience. He said that, because he would like to take certain steps on the path to salvation, he desired counsel and instruction. Otherwise he has already given to the poor a quantity of rice, as abundant compensation for the harm he did his neighbor. He is generous to the poor according to his means, and his living faith therefore shows itself through love to be so fruitful that it is striking to unconverted people. The commandment of God at Exodus 22:1 concerning four and fivefold restitution (and as Zacheus, Luke 19:8, may have done) causes him trouble and sorrow indeed, especially since he cannot seem to remember how much the secretly purloined fruit amounted to and whether he has compensated the poor fourfold.

I sought to show this honest Christian, as well as some others, according to my meager perception: in penitence, through the effect of the Holy Spirit, there arises a righteous hatred of sin, so that one casts it from oneself and seeks to make amends for the harm one has done to one's neighbor, whether it be one person or, according to the character of the circumstances, the poor. I said that the forgiveness of these and other sins, however, and the healing of the wounds to the conscience were to be sought in Jesus Christ alone, the Savior and Sanctifier of poor sinners. At every feeling of misery, one should make one's own, in faith and humility, His hard-won grace, offered and presented even to the most miserable sinners in the gospel, and hold fast to it at every reproach of the conscience and qualm, for Jesus has atoned for all our sins and paid with His blood and death and has won for us righteousness, life, and blessedness in abundance.

If the faith of the penitent sinner grasps the inestimable ransom of Christ and partakes of the forgiveness of sins and of the entire treasure of grace and blessedness from the beginning, then it is impossible for the fruit of faith to be wanting in the manifestation of love for God, oneself, and one's neigbor, rather it goes as the blessed Luther says in his preface to the epistle to the Romans: "He does not ask whether good works are to be done, rather before one asks, he has done them and is always doing them." What is said in the Old Testament here and there about four or fivefold compensation for goods taken or improperly gotten from one's neighbor does not, in my view, have to be so precisely insisted upon. Indeed, if we do carelessly insist upon it publicly with our parishioners we likely arouse in honest souls only unnecessary trouble and unrest, or at least to some degree they will hide behind the law and (at least secretly) seek rest and relief in their manifold compensation. If the fourfold compensation (that, in the Old Testament, must occur instead of punishment) were so precisely and utterly necessary, one would find a decree from the Lord in the gospel or in the epistles of the apostles. Paul speaks of it thus in Ephesians 4:28: "Let him that stole steal no more: but rather let him labour, working with his hands the thing which is good, that he may have to give to him that needeth," etc., for love goes unforced and unyoked, cf. I Timothy 1:9–11, Ezekiel 33:15, where there is also no number.

I like adding the admonition that souls that have burdened their consciences through thievery and because of absence or other cause cannot talk with the offended neighbor about it, shall pray all the more diligently for them so that the heavenly Father for the sake of Christ might abundantly replace for them and their families in soul and body that which was purloined. For of what significance is the intercession of a faithful person? Certainly a great deal, of which all the promises bear witness. This dear man was very happy that timidity did not deter him from disclosing his condition, and he went home with joy and praise of God. I was also happy that God presented me the opportunity to serve this dear man, whose demeanor I find very edifying and blessed, with my office and meager understanding. It is too bad that many people do not wish to come out properly with their scruples! With them comes true what is said in Sirach 41: "One is often ashamed when one should not be ashamed."

Sunday, the 17th of April. Brückner visited me after the afternoon divine services and attested that the Lord had presented him with much mercy in his penitence and faith, so that he knew for certain that He had accepted him to grace for the sake of Christ's merit. He said, however, that often the feeling of God's grace would fade and then his Christianity would begin to falter. For many good souls amongst us it goes thus, so that they place the assurance of God's grace in the perception of it, when nonetheless it is not called believing; and if a few mistakes and transgressions do creep in that are a great cross to them, they then become uneasy and think they have frittered away the priceless favor of God. This man has otherwise been very shy about speaking his opinion plainly when other people sin; but God gave him more joyousness, which bore so much fruit that even with the nagging N. woman, who likes to inveigh against others with her unsound judgment and obvious gossip, keeps it to herself in his presence.

On this Sunday *Misericordia Domini*, on which God gave us indeed much mercy through His word, ten children, to wit, four boys and six girls, were admitted publicly to preparation for Holy Communion. We enjoined them briefly with the verse: "This is a faithful saying; and worthy of all acceptation," etc.,"I obtained mercy;" etc., in which manner it must proceed, we said, with their preparation, if they are to be worthily and profitably admitted to the table of the Lord. The goal of this public acceptance is amongst other things that the members of the congregation know which children are to be prepared through God's word and prayer for this important purpose, and therefore not only the ministers but also the pious parishioners might be helpful on their part for their righteous preparation.

Monday, the 18th of April. Today we held the first edification hour on the plantations by Ebenezer Creek, and during it we repeated something from I Chronicles 23; and we began to examine the 24th chapter. The people had gathered after ten o'clock in Sanftleben's dwelling, which lies almost in the middle of the plantations. God crowned this first hour with perceptible blesssing. I am resolved, with God, to spend an hour here every week if possible for the edification of the parishioners; but in the second hour my dear colleague (who indeed has enough work in the school, with preparation of the children for Holy Communion, and otherwise in the congregation) will relieve me and preach something from God's word to them, which I indicated to the people at the close of the hour. May God support us and grant us His blessing!

Wednesday, the 20th of April. I visited the school on the plantations this morning and admonished the children about the words in I Samuel 2:30 and the examples pertaining to them in this chapter, concerning love and obedience to the divine word, so that the blessing of the fifth commandment will come upon them, etc. I also showed the schoolmaster an easy method for instructing the children collectively by means of pronouncing the biblical verses that they have to recite on Sundays publicly; and by means of my pronunciation I taught them quite quickly the verse: "I have gone away like a lost sheep, seek thy servant", etc. Psalm 119. The man not only keeps good order amongst the children but also applies all his diligence to imparting to them reading and good verses and to repeating the sermons with them. His diligence is becoming right familiar to the parents through the children, and they consider his schoolteaching a great benefaction.

Thursday, the 21st of April. On Sunday Brückner told me that our miraculous Lord had used his physical illness, epilepsy,[5] as a means of chastisement and aid. He had first contracted it years ago and since then often found himself disabled by it. God used it to waken him from the sleep of sin and death and to convert him. Now, he said, it was also a preservative for him against frivolousness and debauchery.[6]

From Lemmenhoffer I learned that he and his wife had again been taken ill with a fever, which redounded to the salvation of their souls. He told me that some time ago God had not only brought him to feel his misery 2 but also had blessed in him on New Year's Day the gospel of Christ the Savior of poor sinners in such a way that his body and soul were refreshed thereby and he was brought to a genuine assurance of the forgiveness of his sins. He said it was for him as for one who is worn out and stiff in all his limbs from heavy labor, who all at once is freed from it and attains new strength. When leaving church, it was very easy and refreshing for him, he said. But the feeling of God's grace and the palpable comfort withdrew from his heart completely, and he found himself in sad circumstances, etc.

This morning Mrs. N. visited me. She too suffers bodily and thereby feels very painfully in her conscience the sins that she had formerly committed merrily and joyfully. From time to time she is so melancholy that she cannot be alone. Her husband traveled to Savannah some days ago, hence she was staying in the meantime with young Mrs. Lackner, who in like manner is making good progress and who disclosed the state of her soul to me.

In my house there was a frail young girl who glorified God for the frailty of her body. She considered that if God had not seized her and held her still beneath this scourge she would not have been drawn away from her stinking vanity and damning conformity to the world and to a true conversion, for she quite often has great pains and epilepsy.[7]

Friday, the 22nd of April. N. often has peculiar cases of misfortune, so that one sees well that God is following right behind him, to pull him from the fire as a burning piece of kindling. He has often begun to do penance; but, whenever he gets the desire and any lightening of his bodily and household circumstances, he has once again walked in the old footsteps of self-assurance and spiritual carelessness. Now God has done almost the same thing to his right hand as to Ernst's,[8] and it seems God will also have to take hold of him right seriously, as He did that other, if it is to come to a conversion for him. I told him and his wife that their petulant ignorance was just as great a sin as other things that are presented to us in scripture as damnable sins. I gave him instructions on how he could be saved from it and from his

whole sinful condition, as indeed some amongst us were as ignorant and wicked as these two people are and nonetheless
brought to rights by the great mercy of the Lord. I cried out to
them: "Be ye not as the horse, or as the mule," etc.

Saturday, the 23rd of April. Yesterday towards evening N.
called me for his wife. She had told my dear colleague her circumstances the day before yesterday and had told me the same a
week ago, but her sins appeared greater and greater to her, in
such a manner that she believed it was all over for her. She
thought she had thrust God's grace away from herself too often,
now there was none there for her. I asked our dear Lord to give
me the right words to speak, and He gave me the verse from
Psalms 130:7: "With the Lord there is mercy, and with Him is
plenteous redemption." When she said her heart was telling her
otherwise, I answered that it made no difference, only what was
here was important. I told her that God said from His heart,
Hosea 11:8, " . . . mine heart is turned within me, my repent-
ings are kindled together." She should hold to that, I said, be
calm and hope that things would progress favorably. I said she
herself must acknowledge that she had the recognition of her
sins not from herself. Hence I told her that the God who gave
her this would not cause her to remain in her sins.

When I considered her penitent, I told her that our dear
Lord's will in me was, to wit, what is found in Isaiah 40:1–2. I
announced to her therefore the forgiveness of her sins in His
name. She told me a week ago that sometimes in her great distress the words from Isaiah 49 would appear to her: "But Zion
said, The Lord hath forsaken me, and my Lord hath forgotten
me," etc. They did reassure her at such times, she said. Hence I
drew her attention once more to those words, and I said that the
Lord Jesus had also drawn her into His hands, for He had
caused them to be nailed through on the cross for her also. The
Lord wished to bless everyone!

Wednesday, the 27th of April. Old Kieffer is not finding in
Carolina (with his son), across from us, what he wished for in the
old days. Hence this evening he disclosed to me his desire, according to God's will, to move right over to us and build a dwelling. Nonetheless, he is considering continuing agriculture on his
land. He has in this matter a good purpose, to wit, to be more in

peace and quiet and to have the opportunity to associate to his edification, with his ministers and other honest Christians. I did not refuse him a house plot, rather I left him the choice and made a few suggestions otherwise.

Thursday, the 28th of April. This morning we distributed with great pleasure the remaining subsidy of the Lord Trustees or the so-called corn-shilling.[9] God is presenting us in our place more than a harvest: for, since the last harvest, money has been distributed, and only a few weeks from now we shall have the wheat, barley, and rye harvest. In August the corn, bean, and rice harvest begins: and who knows what our benevolent Father will cause to happen to us in the meantime in the way of another subsidy or act of benevolence. May He make us all, through His spirit, grateful from our hearts and cause the current real awakening to be not fleeting but well founded and lasting.

Saturday, the 30th of April. In this month of April just now ended we have had almost constant cool weather and therewith right penetrating and fruitful rain, hence the European and local crops as well as the garden vegetables are growing very quickly and beautifully from it.[10]

Because in this year the catechism is publicly discussed Sunday afternoons and the public divine services have to be held also every two weeks at the Zion church, my dear colleague, who preaches there, cannot present his meditation on the catechismal truths at the Jerusalem Church on Sunday. He therefore does it on Saturday in the evening prayer hour; and, because the people from the plantations on the Ebenezer Creek are not present, this presentation takes place for them Tuesdays in the edification hour, when I hold the edification hour on the stories of the Old Testament at the Zion Church. May God bless everything presented from His word and from the catechism in the souls of ourselves and our parishioners!

N., the servant in the orphanage, does not want to come out from the law under which he has lived for some years or to look to the gospel and the grace so abundantly offered to sinners before his eyes, as it were.[11] He feels his corruption, struggles against the flesh and concerns thereof, drills diligently in prayer, and is a great admirer of the divine word and good conversation, as from time to time the gospel penetrates very powerfully into his heart. Nonetheless, he does not wish to grasp, still less can he believe, that God for the sake of Christ wishes to forgive him his sins, which he still feels and must struggle with daily. But, if he could just master his sins and extirpate them, then faith in Christ and acquisition of His meritorious justification would reach him more easily; and he would exchange justification for sanctification. In this I directed him by means of God's word.

M A Y

Tuesday, the 3rd of May. Our people's cattle have till now run loose in the Abercorn area, where on account of the quite splendid meadow a great many cattle habitually stayed. Also those cows are there that soon after our arrival in Abercorn and Old Ebenezer ran away from the first transport and doubtless have multiplied. Because now some men from our congregation have often had to ride across this Abercorn region on account of their cattle and have found it quite fertile indeed for agriculture and cattle breeding, they asked me to look at it myself and apply to our superiors possibly to have it incorporated into our township or into the land appertaining to our city. Now there is only one man and two frail children there and he is accomplishing very little in agriculture, hence he is living in great poverty. Upon our arrival this place (adjacent to the village) was better occupied, but the people either died off or moved away. From this we can see that most of the English and French cannot support themselves on the best land because they do not wish to labor in the field.[1]

Wednesday, the 4th of May. Captain N. of Port Royal, who slandered me and our congretation in Parliament (I reproached him with it in a letter), wrote a very polite letter to me today.[2] In it he explained himself as best he could and excused himself by saying that he did not know better, and believed he had heard such complaints as he cited there from an inhabitant of our place, whom he declined to name. He wrote that he would like to trade with our people if his goods were suitable for us.

Friday, the 6th of May. For some time God has afflicted N.'s house with all sorts of suffering and exceptional occurrences, and he himself recognizes that God the Lord must have His own special motives for it. May He cause him to come to the right paths! God opened his eyes some time ago to recognize himself and how much he still lacks; but he still has to recognize, reject, and accept many things if he wishes to become and remain a true, serious Christian. The ideas of men do not suffice until God Himself gives them the proper vigor.

Saturday, the 7th of May. Yesterday a boat with corn arrived here. Colonel Stephens is sending it to the Englishman in Old Ebenezer for his horses. On this boat there was a barrel of beer, a small keg of syrup, and a large container of sugar. A friend from Savannah wrote me that these things would be sent to me by General Oglethorpe; but, because no further letter arrived to direct me in the use of these things, I do not know what is meant thereby. General Oglethorpe has often presented us with wine, and it seems likely that these handsome gifts, too, come as presents from him; the matter will become clear very soon.

Monday, the 9th of May. If N. would learn to recognize penitently that Christ shed His blood for her, too, He would also speak these words to her: "I, even I, am He that blotteth out thy transgressions for mine own sake, and will not remember thy sins." Finally, I prayed to our dear Lord to help her to that point. She liked everything and she said that she wished I would come again, which she otherwise had not desired. I (Gronau) visited a few more members of the congregation, and I sensed abundantly the support of our dear Savior. I was gladened to hear from one person that she could say she now believed;[3] previously, she said, she was trapped in unbelief. Still another person wished to learn better and better to believe, because she was still lacking so much therein. I spoke with her then about one and another thing that appertained to that. In one's unconverted state one has enough faith, and yet it is only unbelief; but, after one has really come to faith, one sees that one lacks nothing more than true faith, hence it is indeed necessary for one to look upon Jesus the beginner and ender of faith and to fight the good fight of faith.

Tuesday, the 10th of May. At midday around 12:00 I (Boltzius) returned from Savannah, with God's support; I had made the journey down in six hours and back in eight. I spoke to Mr. Jones for the last time before the journey he was to undertake in a week. I was very impressed by his honest attitude and sincere, simple love for me, my dear colleague, and our whole congregation. For a couple of years now he has allowed me the use of his empty house near the landing as a shelter for our people. We have also used it till now for the gatherings of the German people for prayer, performance of holy baptism, and other Christian practices. Because he himself now has guard duty or must deposit some money yearly on the night watches to be held (which comes to a tidy sum), it would have been my obligation to carry this onus or give him a certain house rent, but he would accept nothing, rather he attested his joy that his house was being used in such a good cause and for such a good purpose. He allowed me to use it in the same manner in his absence and said the repairs would cost me nothing. For that I wish for him God's blessing and the House not made by human hands as abundant repayment.

Yesterday evening I held prayer hour on Luke 13:1–9. In it is not only a doubly sad story with the proper application but also a very important allegory of a fig tree in a husbandman's garden that was cultivated, to be sure, but remained unfruitful. I was brought to this text by two depressing events that came to my attention two weeks ago and now once again. The first time, a long boat had capsized, one man had drowned miserably, and the other had been badly mangled on an oyster bed. On Sunday a girl in Savannah was struck dead by lightning at three o'clock in the afternoon at the hearth near the fire. She was buried yesterday with the solemnities customary amongst the English. At this time on Sunday we also had rain and thunderstorms, but the Lord graciously caused it to pass over without harm. The saddest thing about this matter is that only a small, small fraction of the people turn to such admonitions and calls to penitence from God; rather, as Mr. Jones unhappily told me, they engage in foolery and mockery in company with thunder and lightning, whereby even those who occupy important positions damage their character badly. Everything impressed my heart greatly and drove me to God so that on that account I profited right much from this journey.

Friday, the 13th of May. This morning I visited N.N. in order to talk with her somewhat from God's word, for her salvation.

She was lying down quite miserably, could not get up from bed, and from time to time had many pains. Because she has hated me and spoken ill of me I reproached her with the verse from I John 3:15: "Whosoever hateth his brother (rather his minister and spiritual advisor) is a murderer: and ye know that no murderer hath eternal life abiding in him." She acknowledged that she indeed had had a bad attitude like that towards me but no longer. Nonetheless, since the sin had been committed by her, I admonished her to repent it and humbly to beg forgiveness from God. Hereupon I emphasized the verse: "Blessed are they who are pure of heart, for they," etc. with the addition: what is impure and vulgar will not go to heaven.

Although she said that she had an impure heart and had prayed last night "Create in me a clean heart, Oh God," etc., I nonetheless reminded her to trust not herself, as if she recognized her innate and self-made impurities. I said she by herself would be left blind and would no longer know herself to be penitent, as God was giving her to recognize by means of the duties of chastisement of the Holy Spirit. She should consider, I said, how David prays, Psalm 139:23–24: "Search me, O God," etc. I said if he, a very wise king and prophet of the Lord, did not trust his own judgment and did not consider himself cunning and observant, rather surrendered himself to God in prayer as a test of his heart, what should she do? I told her that she had wasted her previous time and spent it badly, and that now she would have to view every moment as precious and constantly lament to God so that He might bring her to penitence and faith, etc.

If her eyes were opened by means of God's mercy, I said, she would no longer say that I had done too much to her, rather she would acknowledge that too little had befallen her; she deserved hell a thousand times over. She liked my speaking and praying with her, and she requested that I pay her another visit, etc. When I began talking with her of temporal things upon which her heart had only recently been set, in order to clear away the offence that she took at me and my judgment, she did not wish to hear much of it, rather she seemed to be quite well satisfied. May God take pity on this poor person who stayed willfully blind in her healthy days and went from one piece of malice to another and who stirred up much scandal.

Saturday, the 14th of May. Because next week Mr. Jones will be
going to Frederica and from there further on via Pennsylvania
to London, I have written once more to him. I thanked him for
the affection shown me, my dear colleague, and our people; and
I commended him to the grace of God on sea and land. I have
consulted with him till now in many things and found his counsel good. This time I transmitted to him a petition that I had
intended to submit to the authorities, but I desired first his *vide-
tur*[4] on it. The content of the writing was this: nine years ago Mr.
Causton had sent us six head of cattle in a small boat at General
Oglethorpe's order. They ran away from our people into the
woods and canebrakes and into Dr. Graham's plantation. The
people could not fetch them back because they lacked fit horses
then and in the time to follow, and they were also unfamiliar
with the woods.

For just this same cause they had had to leave five other cows
that had run away into the same region, without searching for
them or bringing them back. But after they were provided with
horses and came to know the forest better they wished to fetch
and brand the old and young cattle that they had seen partly in
the previous winter in the region behind Abercorn and Dr.
Graham's plantation. To their amazement, however, they became aware that quite many young cows, oxen, and yearling
calves had been branded with a fresh brandmark, but the ears, I
said, had been left whole and unmarked.[5] As the Englishman
and our people in Old Ebenezer reckoned, Dr. Graham did it.
But it would be a hard thing for our inhabitants if they were to
lose the above mentioned young and old cattle that they could
not retrieve on account of the aforementioned causes. The authorities could prevent that by their wise judgment. Hence I am
asking to be advised whether:

1) our people may not by rights claim for themselves the oldest
cows in the region of Abercorn and Dr. Graham's plantation,
those that still have an old Carolina brand and earmark? We do
not know what special mark these gift cattle had that ran away
nine years ago, for they broke loose soon.

2) our people may not by rights claim for themselves a few
young cows, oxen, and yearling calves that in their judgment belong to the old and the other runaway cows?

With the arrival of the 4th transport the worthy Senior Riesch sent to us a fine piece of green linen for drapes for our church windows. It can be very profitably applied now to the Zion Church, where there are still no glass windows. Eight curtains have been finished on four windows, by which means the wind and sunshine will be stopped from inconveniencing the preacher more than with open windows. The second floor has also not yet been laid in this church, and there is a lack of boards for it, hence the preacher carries a much greater burden when preaching than in the Jerusalem Church. We are hoping that God will send us the money and the carpenters in enough time also to finish this construction, to His praise and our edification. It is surely good for us not to receive everything at once, for then we ask all the more for God's Gifts, and when one after the other falls to us from the hand of God we praise Him all the more often.

Monday, the 16th of May. Young Mrs. N. from the 4th transport was powerfully awakened a short time ago and seems now to be seriously concerned about her salvation. She wept copiously this morning when I visited her, upon acknowledging her sins: and she considers herself the greatest sinner and unworthy of every divine blessing. I might wish that N. would look more deeply into himself but he is still more concerned with external things and goes no further than the diligent practice of the means of salvation. Perhaps God can bless, to his awakening, the admonitions that I sought to place in his heart.

Tuesday, the 17th of May. I know from R. St. /Ruprecht Steiner/ that he conversed edifyingly with Mrs. N., and took great pains to bring her to better thoughts. Because she now has especial need of exhortation and instruction and she perhaps has only a short time to live, I asked him this morning if he might visit her from time to time and exhort her from God's word to the advancement of true penitence. He himself has penitence and faith in living experience, and for those who are impenitant or in error he has a special zealous ardor. Nonetheless, he does not merely urge the law, rather he works on his neighbor with compassion and much patience and does not, for that reason, immediately discard him although he finds disagreement and ingratitude. I hope by his service to this poor person at least to learn whether her (till now good) attestations, in words and be-

havior towards me and my dear colleague, are well-founded or
not. For she will open herself self to him more fully than she will
to us; she has done it previously and puts especially great store in
this man.

Friday, the 20th of May. N.N. sent word to me that she would
like to speak with me or my dear colleague concerning the condition of her soul, if only she had the opportunity. I provided an
opportunity to her to come to me, for she attested that she would
like to convert to God but could not; she could not, she said, either pray or think good thoughts. She said she was feeling much
anxiety in her conscience and that it appeared to her that she
was lost because she had rejected the grace of God for so long,
etc. My advice and instruction went as follows: 1) to be diligent in
prayer even if the words did not flow easily and her heart ap-
peard to be tightly closed. But especially, I said, her prayer must
be directed towards properly learning to recognize the abyss of
her corrupted heart and to come to salutary regret and proper
contrition. For "the sacrifices which please God," etc. 2) she
should ponder diligently the small and very important little
word "faithfulness" and seek to practice it in her waking ac-
tivities and in prayer. I said that the kingdom of God started
small in the soul and for that reason was compared with a mus-
tard seed. "To him who hath, shall it be given." etc. 3) she should
keep company with Christian women even if there were only a
few of them, and not stifle and deny the first grace for fear of
people.

Sunday and Monday, the 22nd and 23rd of May were the celebration of Holy Pentecost. Praise God who in this celebration has
granted us not only bodily health and pleasant weather for the
observance of it but has also sent us much grace for edification to
eternity. It can also be said in our case, from Acts 9:31, "Then
had the churches rest throughout all Judea and Galilee and Sa-
maria, and were edified; and walking in the fear of the Lord,
and in the comfort of the Holy Ghost, were multiplied." Hallelujah! For our Saturday's preparation we had the important text
from Luke 13:1 ff. and were admonished by our dear Savior
most sincerely and affectionately to apply this holy celebration
to our true betterment before the judgments that are already ap-
proaching overtake them, as with the impenitent and unfaithful

Jews. I intended to close sooner the present story of the Levites
and thereupon to recite in a prayer hour my meditation on the
aforementioned remarkable histories and the appended comparison with Luke 13. God, however, reserved them for us until
the last hour shortly before the celebration, and then they were
especially appropriate for us.

Tuesday, the 24th of May. Ruprecht Steiner called on me during the celebration, and during our conversation he came to his
current state of body and soul. He said his body was getting
weaker and weaker; and, because his fieldwork was therefore
getting more and more toilsome and he had to apply a great deal
of time to keeping the grass from spreading too much, he got so
tired working that in the evenings he could not hold spiritual
sessions with his family as long and as seriously as previously.
This was causing him great concern, he said, and it appeared
that he was regressing in his Christianity. I told him that his labor, if it took place in faith and love of God, was pleasing to God
and was a divine service.[6] I reminded him of the didactic poem
about the hermit who saw that a maid in an inn was leading a
better Christian life than he: she had had no special practice except to remember her crucified Savior during all her rough
work and sincerely to thank Him for love, etc. I said that, because he was fatigued in the evening and hence could not keep
up prayer and reading, it did not take away from his Christianity, for before God it did not depend on long prayer but
rather penitent and faithful prayer. I told him that he should
consider what the late Luther wrote about morning and evening
prayer in the catechism: if only a prayer such as that were ut-
tered with contrite and faithful heart, one would be able to practice what was in the passage: "Then fall asleep quickly and
joyfully."

Old Rieser had a very painful bodily occurrence, but nonetheless he was able to attend divine services during the days of celebration and take something along for his illness. Today I found
him troubled in his mind, and he was also weeping over the fact
that for two years he had taken pains to convert to God and had
also felt much grace in his heart but had been unable to come to
a proper certainty of the state of grace. I told him that his in-
constancy was to blame; for, because he did not gird himself with

prayer, things could easily get in his way about which he had become angry and deceived or upset himself. In this way the grace and good intentions once more, if not lost, had nonetheless had grown very weak. He could not deny it; and his wife, weeping copiously, corroborated it with several examples. Now the Lord was not only grasping his body but was also stirring his conscience powerfully, so that he felt his misery and longed for the free grace in Christ. I emphasized for him the precious verse that we heard yesterday: "God, Our Savior, will have all men be saved and come to knowledge," etc.

Thursday, the 26th of May. Yesterday evening after the prayer hour a sick woman with three already grown children, to wit, two sons and a daughter, came to us from Purysburg and requested to be taken care of spiritually and physically. They have been ill for quite some time and for that reason have been reduced to the utmost poverty. They claimed that they were weary of life in Purysburg and wished to be in Ebenezer not only in their days of sickness but also in their days of health and to settle into a life of all good order. The children are ignorant,[7] and it is their and their mother's wish to be instructed in salutary doctrine.

Because there is otherwise no opportunity here to shelter poor, sick people, we have had to resolve to take them into the orphanage where they are provided with food and drink, a good bed, and necessary assistance, but chiefly with Christian instruction and exhortation. Although the opportunities are quite constrained in the orphanage and our supplies for bodily care of people entrusted to us are small, I still could not refuse to accept in love these suffering strangers who otherwise, as they themselves confess, would have to perish in body and soul. What we do not have in physical means for the care of these people, the almighty Creator of heaven and earth, our dear Father reconciled in Christ can easily cause to fall to us.

It is not to be looked upon as an accident that this morning, when the acceptance and care of these strangers lay on my mind, a letter from Mr. Newman including a very cordial and edifying note from beneficent merchants from V. was delivered to me.[8] Among other things they reported the following: "We are only instruments by which our dear Lord caused these meager gifts to reach you in Ebenezer the last time. By the same means once more 10 pounds Sterling are coming to you that we have caused to be paid to Mr. Newman in London with today's mail, beseeching him to remit the same to you. Therefore you may be pleased to apply this small gift either to the benefit of the orphanage or to other persons in poverty and need from their congregation according to your pleasure and discretion; we leave to you the complete disposition thereof."

Ah! a wise God who does everything that is fine in His time. It was also indicated in the close of the letter that another gift of two pounds for us had been appended to this handsome one for the orphanage or the pressing need of the poor. May the Lord cause these His precious instruments and their worthy families to be abundantly rewarded in soul and body, for this as well as all else that has flowed down upon us and our congregation these last few years from this little fountain, and may he cause them once more to find a blessed fruit from this well-spread seed in blessed eternity.

Friday, the 27th of May. It is most appropiate that we are receiving the edifying letter from the blessed merchants from V. just now when we are bringing to an end the pertinent story of the Levites from I Chronicles 24–28 in the prayer and edification hours and began profiting from the story from I Kings 1. It turned out just that way before our last memorial and thanksgiving celebration, and at that time the letters from Europe came to us right apropos in like manner. We guided ourselves therefore according to God's sign and took great profit from the abovementioned letters before the Lord in yesterday's evening prayer meeting. We were awakened anew from them to copious praise of God, spiritual joy, and a heartfelt intercession for these and other worthy benefactors.

With God's blessing a similar thing is to take place today during the edification hour in the Zion Church, and it is part of the bliss of Ebenezer that not only are many practicing Christians praying for us and praising God about us but are also working on us from afar by means of edifying communications.

In our letter of 15 January of last year we gave these dear benefactors the short report that God had presented us with a church. Who would have thought at the time that, after we received an answer to this letter, we would have a second church belonging to Ebenezer and that in both churches we would find in their letter material for edification and intercession, as is now happening? We also wrote in the above-mentioned letter to the same persons these details: "Our orphanage is proceeding constantly with blessings, and the Lord is giving us quite much evidence that it is being established in His name and is being carried out in His honor and for salvation of the widows and orphans, indeed of the whole congregation, and N.B. we are hopeful by and by for the salvation of other persons in this country." Who could have guessed that we would receive their reply to it and their loving gift specified in it in such circumstances, when our miraculous and gracious God began so clearly to fulfill our hope, as is mentioned under yesterday's entry. We replied joyfully yesterday to their letter, which was so pleasing to us; and we reported something of the miraculous and, as it were, simultaneously effortless wisdom and kindness of God with us.

Saturday, the 28th of May. Mrs. Bischoff has been in the orphanage for a few weeks now, and our kind Lord has begun a good work in her soul.[9] For this reason she has become very fond of the orphanage, and would perhaps like to spend her time constantly in it if the circumstances of her household did not require otherwise. Her husband requested that she come home once more, as he had much work and needed her help. He recognizes the great benefaction that has redounded to her, his helpmeet, by her being accepted into the orphanage, since otherwise, as he said, her health and existence would have come to grief.

When I visited the four sick people from Purysburg today, I found N.N. in an adjoining room on her knees. She has often retired there to sing and pray. I told her briefly what she would have to do to be more and more established in received grace. There are some people present in the congregation who have been driven into the orphanage by their bodily distress. God has supplied them there with spiritual relief along with the physical relief, which is a comfort to me, especially whenever I have to see that the purpose of this little establishment is not blessed in everyone who enjoys the many good things in it.

The only thing we lack here is a single Christian person who would constantly have guardianship over the children and other people who have business here; but this requires a person of good qualities and Christian experience, otherwise more harm than profit arises. I was told by the four sick people from Purysburg that previously they had had much prejudice against our office and congregation and acted the part of slanderers. Today, however, I told them that we would preach on nothing but the narrow path that leads to life. Because three of them could read, I said, whenever they shall be able to come to church they are to bring along their Bibles or New Testaments and diligently consult what is preached to them, for our parishioners are directed to nothing other than God's word. Except for it, they must believe nothing concerning spiritual matters and things pertaining to blessedness.

Sunday, the 29th of May. N. called on me and was very sad and downcast; she considers herself very evil and not worthy of one single benefaction of God, on the contrary worthy of every curse and damnation. Whatever good things are told her from the gospel do not stick, and she cannot believe that she can partake of it at all because she is not only very evil but also impenitent and unfaithful. Because time was short I told her a little about the two verses: "Come unto me all ye who," etc. and "Blessed are the poor in spirit, for theirs is the kingdom of heaven." The afternoon divine services were starting immediately, in which my dear colleague was preaching precious evangelical truths about the first part of the interpretation of the 2nd article of the Christian faith, and therefore I hope that God raised her troubled and downcast spirit even more.

Monday, the 30th of May. We indicated yesterday that in two weeks, on the Second Sunday after Trinity, we shall hold Holy Communion, for which young Mrs. N. already reported today in private. God is letting her recognize the depth of her corruption but is also disclosing to her the depths of His grace, but in the meantime its feeling and taste are disappearing, so that she is vascillating and hesitating once again. And, because she is still not right firm, she is worrying that she may perhaps, as has happened at other times, go 'to the Lord's table to her own detriment. I recited the verse to her "They that be whole need not a physician, but they that are sick," etc. The Lord Jesus welcomes sinners who are penitent and hungry for grace; if we did not have and did not feel distress and misery we would need no savior, no spiritual medicine, and no communion. I learned from someone that she was living quite contentedly with her husband on their plantation and that she considers it a benefaction of God to be in this wilderness. Her husband labors diligently; and, although she cannot help in agriculture, she nonetheless makes much profit for herself and him with her needle, for the people bring them all sorts of tailoring and women's work.

Tuesday, the 31st of May. Pichler disclosed to me this morning that God blessed yesterday's evening prayer hour in such a way that he recalled old sins of his youth, and his heart was filled with divine sadness over it. He was amazed at the divine kindness that had drawn him this time right into the prayer hour, when otherwise it would have been his wife's turn and he would have had to remain home with his sick children. We made our beginning by observing the things that befell dear David in the last days of his life, from I Kings 1. We heard that this dear man in his old age still had a severe illness to endure in which he lost his strength in such a way that he did not keep his natural warmth and was quite cold in all his extremities. In his youth and his manly age David was very vigorous, spirited, and active; but he had many toilsome labors to endure in his father's house with the sheep as well as later at the time of Saul and his regime, and as regent and master on many occasions he could not save his strength, etc. How refreshing it must have been to him on his sick bed to remember that in his youth and adulthood he had expended his strength in the service of his God and for the benefit of his neighbor. On the other hand the memory of the opposite may have been a hell to his waking conscience.

Strength of body and spirit are great gifts of the Lord; one can indeed recognize that when one lacks them, even if only one member is crippled. But the abuse of such noble powers must also be a very great sin, one in which a great many people are fixed and do no penance for it. Many people dissipate their strength in openly sinful behavior and desire, I Peter 4:2,3; and, when they offer the blossom of their age to the devil and the dregs of it to God, they invite the curse upon their necks, cf. Ecclesiastes 11:9, 12:1. When others have spent their strength, they have a better appearance, for they labor, worry, fret, and grieve almost to death, etc. Again others exalt their bodily strength; and they sin through self-love when they should consider that they do not have it from themselves but from God, who can take it away from as quickly as He can give it. A small illness takes away fine figure, strength, and life. By that we impressed upon them the verse Jeremiah 9:23–24. We gave our diligent laborers something from this as well as from the recently examined story from I Chronicles 28:26 ff. in the way of economical admonitions; and we shall note something here from it for the next time.

JUNE

Wednesday, the 1st of June. To get some exercise this morning I traveled to a Salzburger's plantation. During the trip I met a woman and I asked her where she was. It was clear to her that my question concerned something spiritual, hence she drew nearer to me and told me that she now had to believe that God loved her, for during the last Pentecost holy day, she said, the Lord had accepted her heart sincerely and had forgiven her everything. I was pleased by this and admonished her to remain with Jesus and to let nothing, even the feeling of sin, make her turn away from Him.

Thursday, the 2nd. of June. When I began the short trip that is now ending, the verse occurred to me: "God's kindness endures forever," and to His glory I must now say that this great undeserved kindness of the Lord on this journey became right specially recognized and new. We departed Tuesday evening, but on the water between here and Purysburg we came into peril several times because my current oarsman had slight experience with boat and water travel. At my sighing, our divine Father granted me in Purysburg a large boat laden with meat. I boarded it; and around eleven o'clock I continued my journey quite comfortably and safely with my own small boat following along behind. After four o'clock in the morning we reached Savannah; and, after reading a beautiful pensum[1] from holy scripture and mutual prayer with my traveling companions, I had hardly gotten onto the street when someone brought the news that Col. Stephens had received new information from England, etc.

My journey was also profitable this time in that I was able not only to baptize a pair of twins—their mother had died shortly after they were born because she lacked a knowledgeable mid-wife—but also because I learned at one time of three families of German people for whom the word of God had seemed barren till now, in whose hearts by means of our humble office it was sown and awakened right powerfully, and bloomed beautifully. Because everything in Savannah went as well as I might possibly have wished, I worried that God might cause me to be humbled on my return journey by means of an unfortunate occurrence. But it did not happen. Rather, although the boat was almost overloaded and, on account of the lack of space, I had to leave a man behind in Savannah until the larger boat arrived and had to row myself, nonetheless it went so rapidly and quite without obstacles that, as I hoped, it was being borne and carried out by the angels. Hence this evening we sang in the prayer hour: "Praise the Lord, who dearly blesses thy condition, who rains streams of love from heaven, think of what the Almighty can do, who confronts thee with love,"[2] cf. Genesis 24:12.

Friday, the 3rd. of June. I formerly wished for *Statii Lutherus Redivivus*,[3] but now we are receiving indeed the most highly profitable and edifying extracts from the writings of our precious Luther.[4] For this great benefaction that redounds not only to our benefit but also to the benefit of members of our congregation (because of the copious numbers of copies sent), may God abundantly bless our cherished Superintendent Lindner and find for him a reward of grace before His throne. The *Little Treasure Chest*,[5] so many copies of which have been sent to us, will, as I have already perceived today, cause much joy and praise of God in desirous and spiritually hungry souls. I know that they need them in order to be led better and better into the living source of the word of God, from which everything has flowed there, and to waken their hearts to faith and obedience on days when, on account of dealings in their trades, they perhaps cannot get to reading their Bibles.

Saturday, the 4th of June. After yesterday's edification hour on the plantations, Mrs. N. explained to me the distress in her soul and conscience and that being alone was harmful to her. She said she could not resist wicked thoughts, hence she had sought the company and help of young Mrs. N. in her prayers. I spoke to her briefly in her weakness of body and conscience from God's word, took away her notion that her sins were greater than God's grace, and acquiesced in her desire once more to move to the orphanage if it could take place with the agreement of her husband. Today she came also into the city and to the orphanage with young Mrs. N., with whom she had bound herself for one purpose in the Lord. The two of them visited me and N. asked once more if she might have permission, although she saw herself as indeed the greatest sinner, to take Holy Communion immediately. She began to disclose the wounds of her conscience, lamented the bad company she had kept in Germany and how she had sinned by means of arrogance and profanation of the Lord's day and by other coarse ways. I noted that she would gladly have poured out much from her conscience but I interrupted her since it was not timely, N. being present, and the harm from it could perhaps be greater than the profit. I hope that God will carry out the good work that He has begun in these two souls gloriously, so that joy will arise from it in heaven and on earth.

Sunday, the 5th of June. Yesterday at noon some people gathered at our office to ask of our merciful Lord much grace from the abundance of our great Savior as a rich reward for His worthy instruments in Halle, Augsburg, London, V.,[6] Saalfeld, and wherever they might be, and sincerely and humbly to bring Him praise and glory in Jesus Christ's name, for the spiritual and physical benefactions shown us thus far, especially the very pleasing letters, medications, books, and linen. This evening we also had a prayer hour in which a similar thing took place, and we must not doubt our desires have been granted, if we consider the precious and most assured promises. We must just be quite amazed at the great kindness of God which still holds sway over us. Transportation by sea is now very perilous and many things are lost at sea or often quite near land as a result of Spanish tricks; yet the letters and things directed to us, that were also packed in the two crates, arrived safely, so that we could perceive not the slightest damage.

Tuesday, the 7th of June. We are learning from all the letters that our friends in England and Germany are supposing that our packages had been on those ships that had been so frequently seized by the enemy on their return journey to England, and hence were lost. But, since our miraculous and kind God held His hand over them as well as over the letters and boxes from Halle, their faith and our faith was very much strengthened in the God who rules in the midst of His enemies and who bears everything by means of His mighty word. It is an easy thing for Him to bring hither in a well-preserved condition the gifts that were on their way to us from Halle and Augsburg.

An especial example of faith that is active through love was strongly impressed into our minds: a Christian woman, who is a friend of ours and served earlier and now pursues her own calling of caring for the ill, is reported to have saved 49 Reichsthaler and 12 Groschen from her service and to have dedicated it to the most suffering persons in our congregation. It has recently been reported that a sickbay will be built amongst us and that such an institution is urgently needed. Perhaps the Lord wishes also by means of this gift and the attendant impressive circumstances to give us a new sign and impetus. May Jesus from His most gracious, transfigured mouth cause us also to hear the comforting words, Matthew 25:34: "Come, ye blessed . . . I was sick and ye visited me . . . ".

This evening in the prayer hour we profited from the edifying contents of the letter from Court Chaplain Ziegenhagen, of 8 February of this year; and we heard much from it for our instruction and comfort. It is quite necessary for us to be reminded again and again of the Spanish invasion (as happens also in this letter). We cannot consider the great kindness of God, if there is but one drop of Christian blood in us, without amazement and joy, as it held sway over us at that time so especially clearly. Everything was in commotion in the country: yet we did not lose our footing at all, so to speak, rather we sat in our fortress, safe and comforted, which at that time was called the name of the Lord and shelter of the Most High, Psalms 91. And, when our loving and Almighty God proceeded to do great miracles of His kindness and power for our little band, as the diaries indicate, and to which pertains the miraculous protection of the letters and things sent here in this perilous time of war, we may conclude and hope that He intends something good for Ebenezer. Perhaps many honest souls in Germany who see simply thick clouds of spiritual and physical judgment over and around themselves, wish what David wished, Psalms 55:7, "O, that I had wings like a dove," etc.

Wednesday, the 8th of June. Yesterday during the edification hour and today during the prayer hour we cheerfully invited our parishioners to gather this afternoon in the Jerusalem Church for the distribution of the books and linen received from Halle. I reminded them that no one should avoid the transaction because he might think that his turn may not come up in this distribution, or he might receive only a meager portion that could as easily be sent to him as for him to have received it himself. I told them herewith the well-known German catch phrase: "Who scorns the lesser shall also lack the greater." For, as we recognize from the current letters, there are still more physical blessings on their way for us, which God can as easily take back as grant, if we do not handle the present ones faithfully, thankfully, and humbly. In addition, many poor people do not understand what the greater purpose is with our distribution, to wit, the spiritual blessings that are presented to us from the abundance of grace of Jesus Christ: we seek always to hallow the gifts we have received for distribution by song, prayer, and preaching of God's word.

It is also especially appropriate in this for us to have the opportunity mutually to praise God the giver of all good and welcome gifts for all His benefactions that He has bestowed spiritually and physically on Ebenezer and to pray for our precious benefactors. I remembered that a year ago at this time, to wit, on the 6th of June, we celebrated holy Pentecost. At that time God offered us the gifts from the gospel that Christ rendered unto us and presented them to those who were penitent and hungry for grace; and now He is causing us to hold a pleasing distribution of spiritual and physical benefactions (to wit, very edifying books, linen, and, above all, great blessings for edification from the letters), which should indeed be justly joyful for us. This morning towards ten o'clock we gathered in great numbers in the Jerusalem Church. Along with me old and young, men, women, and children gave voice to the beautiful song: *Was gibst du denn, O meine Seele,* etc. After the prayer I took up once more this arousing song of devotion and showed briefly from it what good things our loving God had given us as well as what we should give Him once more in return. Amongst the physical benefactions that the Lord has bestowed on us:

1) That God is causing us to hold a distribution at the time when the Spanish invasion is almost a year past. A year ago it was also thus, by which means He wished to strengthen our faith in Him the living God; He had no desire to extirpate us, rather to plant us, build us, settle us, and fortify us so that the gates of hell could not overpower us, if by means of penitence and faith we cause ourselves to be brought properly to Christ.

2) That till now God has graciously spared us from the illnesses with which a year ago the 4th transport was afflicted; Instead of attacking us, He wishes to lead us to penitence through His goodness, which is revealed by this distribution. Anyone who scorns this kindness need not be surprised if God comes in earnest and seeks thereby to rescue him like a brand from the fire.

3) I requested the parishioners to consider quietly the expression in the above-mentioned hymn, "God, who daily giveth thee everything,"[7] *Quot verba, tot pondera,*[8] "You," you unworthy sinner, "daily," (for His kindness is renewed every day), "everything", everything that is profitable in body and soul, indeed not just the necessities, rather He gives everything abundantly and in great profusion. His grace is incomprehensible, like a great torrent of water, etc., and what comprises the little word "giveth", not per se, if we reflect upon the sublime Giver and His glorious and comforting characteristics, and also our own circumstances. In the third and fourth verse of the above-mentioned hymn the precious benefactions of the second and third articles of Christian faith are brought home to us. On Sundays my dear colleague preaches on them in order, and to the hearts indeed God grants so much; and if the parishioners do not resist, places them in their hearts. What we now

II) should give back to God is indicated by the entire content of the above-mentioned hymn, and there are also right rousing emotional grounds in it for compelling us to a willing surrender of our hearts. Afterwards, when we had knelt and praised God

for every good thing and had prayed for ourselves and our benefactors, the distribution proceeded with the adults of the entire
congregation in such a manner that amongst sixty-two adults
and thirty-two children of the first and last transports were distributed handsome pieces of linen, and amongst the two middle
transports were distributed Superintendent Lindner's extracts
from Dr. Luther's Postille, books, Bibles, hymnbooks, and *Little
Treasure Chests,* all in good order.[9] The three first transports received the linen from Halle a year ago, and the last transport
received books; now the last transport was being supplied with
linen, which fell also to the people of the small first transport,
both of which transports on the contrary this time received no
books. We are glad to see to it that each and every member of the
congregation has some part and joy in the distribution.

Friday, the 10th of June. I called on Ruprecht Steiner and
talked with him and her[10] about the composition and blessedness of faith; and I said that for a faithful person everything,
even his previous and present sins and crimes, must serve his
benefit. He had dug a well in his yard and gone to a great deal of
trouble but had been unable to find any water. It is already over
25 feet deep but has clay to halfway down and thereafter pure
yellow sand. He would like to dig deeper but looks on the dig-
ging as perilous because the sand round the sides falls down and
might entomb the digger. He is also worried that he still would
not get water unless he dug as deep as the Mill Stream, which
would make over fifty feet. May God be willing to direct this
dear man to the proper method so that his many labors may
come to the desired goal!

The water in the Mill Stream and the Savannah is falling day
by day and is getting very low. The dry, arid weather has lasted
quite long, the heat has been very great both day and night; and
we urgently require a penetrating and refreshing rain so that
the fruits and vegetables in the fields and gardens will not spoil.
The little streams and holes where the livestock were accustomed to drink in the woods have dried up, and that forces
the cattle, as is being said, into such areas where they can find
water. Anyone who has business in the woods must not go too far
because there is practically no water to be found anywhere. May
God take pity on our need but teach us to hold the benefaction

of water and rain in proper high regard and practice what it says in Psalm 123: "Unto thee lift I up mine eyes, O thou that dwellest in the heavens. Behold, as the eyes of servants, etc., so our eyes wait upon the Lord our God, until that he have mercy upon us."

This evening and morning, God willing, I am considering finishing the sharing of the blessings from the beautiful letters, so that next week we will be able to continue our observations in the Bible story, according to God's will. Such a pleasant change of pace is very profitable for us. Our pious parishioners are reading the reports from Prussia together in small groups, and what I have especially to make known to them about their countrymen will take place partly in my house and partly before and after the edification hours on the plantations.[11]

Saturday, the 11th of June. This time a few replies from Prussia arrived to the inquiries of our Salzburgers, but thereby their desire has not been quieted because many are still lacking and we hope shall be sent along in the future. A couple of Salzburg schoolmasters wrote quite cordially to some of their acquaintances in our congregation, which we hope will have a good impression and profit.

Sunday, the 12th of June. This afternoon it was very hot, which was somewhat burdensome for us at the divine services. Thunderclouds built up and it seemed as if it might rain heavily, but hardly a few drops fell. Thereby God showed us the benefaction of the rain; it may have rained much in other regions but from us He withdrew it once more, which we cannot look upon as accidental. Yesterday evening, as we read the last letters aloud, we were forcefully reminded that almost all these letters we have received have mentioned the Spanish invasion and God's miraculous help for us, and it cannot possibly have happened to no purpose that this important matter was brought home to us freshly again from many places just at the time when the invasion is a year old. God's purpose thereby is without doubt for us, with the support of the Holy Spirit, to make up for what we and many under us have neglected for the entire year. Such a benefaction that God manifests to us not in thoughts, good words, and intentions but rather in deeds, requires also a sincere and active gratitude, which presupposes a virtuous devotion of the heart. If this gratitude is absent and the people in this country and also in our place proceed into frivolousness and self-assurance, we may worry that God will come with new punishments. He has the rod and the sword.

Monday, the 13th of June. A God-seeking woman visited me for edification. I opened up for her the verse on page 118 of the golden *Little Treasure Chest*:[12] "Delight thyself also in the Lord, and he shall, . . . " etc. With that she said that her little girl had wanted to hear that verse from me at the distribution, but that an obstacle had arisen. When I came to Leimberger's house a widow expressed thanks for the *Little Treasure Chest* received at the distribution; and she told me that before leaving the house she had opened up the little verse: "Delight thyself also in the Lord, and He shall give," etc. I was deeply impressed that people were so often reciting this little verse to me. Our parishioners who have now received the *Little Treasure Chest* are greatly pleased, and they have cause for it, for there is a great treasure therein. Some would rather have left the linen to others and for it chosen such booklets. Also the hymnbooks that we distributed to them have been very dear to them, hence we wish that God might move our benefactors immediately to cause to come to us the extract from the beautiful Freylinghausen hymnbook, so that we could share a copy with every single person, big and little.[13]

Tuesday, the 14th of June. Around four o'clock this morning our gracious Lord manifested great mercy to my dear colleague and his house when He graciously delivered his dear helpmeet and gladdened both parents with a healthy and well-formed little daughter.[14] My household along with me and all honest members of the congregation partook sincerely in that joy: and we glorify the Lord for this great mercy, which we also did today in public gathering.

God has heard in grace our poor supplication for our entire parched out ground and has sent us this evening a very drenching, fruitful rain. We accept it from His gentle hand as a treasured gift and we humbly glorify Him for it. There was severe thunder with it, but it passed quite without harm in our region. With this fruitful rain for which we have hoped so long we may also say: "If He doth not help at every time, at least He helpeth when there is need."[15]

Wednesday, the 15th of June. When today I scrutinized the edifying reports of the righteous Archpriest Dr. Schumann[16] on the internal and external circumstances of the Salzburgers in his and the neighboring parish, I found some more replies to the inquiries of our Salzburgers. God bless dear Mr. Schumann for the love and care he has for our congregation and cause him to engender much good still further for the propagation of His kingdom. We were very impressed that by virtue of Dr. Francke's account of the previous year, our dear Lord delivered into the hands of the worthy Archpriest Mr. Schumann twenty-two Reichsthalers or thirty-three Gulden that he sent to Dr. Francke for the benefit of the Salzburger congregation at Ebenezer, although he has around and near him many needy Salzburgers, as I have seen from the reports of Pastor Breuer.[17] Thus His love is impartial and seeks to serve not only indigenous but also foreign poor; indeed it bears the entire world on its heart and would gladly effect good everywhere.

This loyal laborer in the vinyard of the Lord arranged for Salzburgers of both sexes who are under his spiritual care to present to our Salzburgers an edifying account and various very lovely letters, for which we say heartfelt thanks. How much good will our dear Lord cause to come to our ears and eyes from Prussia? We have received a blessed impression what has been reported to us of the circumstances of Dr. Schultz[18] and his schools, which is an obvious work of God and a sign of grace for the Prussian country in these trying times.

A young girl, troubled and downcast, came to me and confessed amidst much weeping that she had wounded and disquieted her conscience by stealing a peach, and for that reason she could not eat or work. I recounted to her what I had just read today in Pastor Breuer's report from Lithuania about an unmarried woman from Salzburg who had found an iron nail on the street and sold it. Soon thereupon her conscience was turbulently awakened and it reproached her with a second, already old, sin of injustice and brought her practically to desperation. If the sin that has been so easily committed awakens in the conscience it burns there like hellfire and gnaws like a raging dog, and then the distinction between great and small sins falls away. From this example she could also learn that God sometimes uses a fresh although small piece of thievery to stir up the remaining evil in the heart, so that the sinner should recognize, I said, the whole chaos of sin, regret it, and beg forgiveness from God for the sake of Christ. I had her recite to me the verse: "If we recognize our sins, then He is true and just and forgives us our sins," etc.

Thursday, the 16th of June. At my request it was proposed to the authorities in Savannah this morning that cows should be given to the former indentured servants of the Lord Trustees, of whom five families are at our place, as well as to the fourth transport and, indeed, to the six poorest families, for which purpose I had to travel to Old Ebenezer before daybreak. I am now very happy to have made the trip because all at once a great deal could be arranged for the benefit of our congregtion by means of God's blessing.

1) the above-mentioned people received eleven cows, herded to our place with their calves very easily by two servants of the Lord Trustees with the assistance of our people. I hope that Col. Stephens will soon receive full authority to give cows to the entire fourth transport. In the meantime I am happy that the poorest got the six cows and as many calves in advance. I would have to pay for them, however, if the Lord Trustees were to alter the resolution addressed to me, but in no way do I suspect that.

2) The two Englishmen who wished to dispute with our people about the recently bought cattle which are grazing with ours were in Ebenezer. I finally persuaded them before witnesses to leave us undisturbed from now on. And therefore I can be relieved of the complaint before the authorities. In this matter our people have a great advantage, if God gives His blessing.

3) Dr. Graham, into whose region our runaway cows go—and he is said already to have branded a few young cattle belonging to us—promised us, with our people present, to assist us with them. He also sold to our people a few cows and young bulls that were partly brought along today with the others, for just the fair price for which I bought the oft-mentioned cattle of a man who died, in Savannah.

4) One of the members of the council in Savannah, along with myself, looked at the sawn boards and other wood lying in Ebenezer.[19] I wished to use it for the sickbay to be built, in case

they wish to make a gift of it to me. He told me that Col. Stephens was now inclined to give it to me and suggested that I bring
the boards and other wood here to Ebenezer. Nonetheless, the
Lord Trustees would rather it be used profitably than left to rot,
for it is lying in the open air.

Monday, the 20th of June. This time in Savannah God sent me
(Boltzius) much that was sweet and joyful: souls awakened from
their sleep of sin were strengthened by the word of the gospel,
and others were thereby attracted. Men of whom one could otherwise have the least hope, deeply entangled partly in coarse
ignorance and great depravity, partly in their own self-justifica-
tion and piety, have become freed from such bonds of Satan.
Hallelujah! Following the afternoon divine services, when I was
rather fatigued, God refreshed me by means of a long, very
pleasant letter from Pastor Muhlenberg in Philadelphia. I now
have a desire to preach to the people and to be in their company.

Friday, the 24th of June. The men have gotten together, now
that the water is low, to get the mill in such a condition that it can
also perform when the water is low. It will cost much labor again,
to be sure, but the profit will also be very great. God give them
further Christian unity and constancy! May it be God's desire
also to awaken Christian hearts in Europe who will cause something to flow to us from their physical blessings for this important construction. We need assistance. If the flour mill is put into
a good, durable condition, to which end the construction people
are getting more and more experience, I would wish that they
would proceed to the building of a rice mill, almost as necessary
to us as the former. By this means our inhabitants would be encouraged to plant more rice than they need for their own necessities, so that by and by we could trade the surplus to others, with
God's blessing. For the last two years we have had no rice planted
at the orphanage because we lack a machine to make the rice
edible and salable. Using people for it costs too much; we would
rather use them at the plow for wheat, rye, barley, and oats, of
which our dear Lord this time has bestowed upon the orphanage such heaps that upon looking at them I was very much
pleased and praised God for it.

The wheat cultivated with the plow has bigger and better
looking kernels than the other with which the people have only

used the hoes. We would wish to have more plows in the congregation, but here in this country no plowshares prepared with iron-hammers are to be had, hence I must write to Mr. Muhlenberg for that reason.[20] If necessary we will drum up two plows. Often I have taken the trouble with all my might to persuade the entire congregation that the householders should transfer soon from the hoe to the plow, whereby they would have much easier labor and great profit. I hope it will soon come to that point, and on account of our orphanage we are considering with God's support to lay out a plantation in the piney woods, especially since everyone is convinced that there will be very useful land there if one applies oneself to making fertilizer, which is quite feasible indeed if one gets more straw from German crops.[21]

Lemmenhofer and Zimmerebner, two diligent and thrifty Salzburgers, wish to dedicate themselves to the orphanage, just as Kalcher has done. We hope that profit can be engendered by their service to others in the congregation who themselves still cannot procure plows, horses, and oxen. It saddens me that men and women labor with the hoe at their corn and beans so often in the greatest heat and have to cut down the grass that is almost ineradicable. By doing this they dissipate their powers before their time, become sick and old; and, when they die, their widows are not in a position to carry on their husbands' plantations tions because a day's wages using the hoe is much greater than the profit. On the other hand, when the plow is used, the deep-rooted grass is easily eradicated, and a single man with a pair of oxen can cultivate more in one day than ten people with the hoe can do otherwise. If they apply themselves to European crops the field is tilled only in fall and winter when there is no great summer heat.

In the spring they would have more time to devote themselves working at sericulture in the shade and otherwise to serve their neighbor with their labor to earn a little money. If they wished to plant corn and beans, it could also take place ten times more easily with the plow than with the hoe. Their so-called good land, upon which oak, walnut, and other deciduous trees grow, is primarily to blame for the fact that they have not till now come to this easy method of farming. That land is full of thick roots that do not rot over several years and therefore let no plow into the earth. In the pine forests it would be much easier, for the roots begin to rot in the first year already, as soon as the trees are cut down. Also there are few such roots, so that one can plow soon in the second year. If the people had applied themselves soon at the beginning to making fertilizer, as is done in Germany, especially when they had the cattle in their stalls, many pine forests would already have been made fertile, by which they would have much advantage and superiority over the so-called good land that is the poorest anyhow.

There are no bears, squirrels, and raccoons in the pine wood that scratch out the corn and gobble it up when it is ripe; they also never have to worry about flooding, as with the low-lying land, or that excessive rain will saturate the crops. If a field has become too old and grassy, it is hardly difficult to lay out other fields in such a pine forest, when the finest hay can be made several times a year on the old one. Our pine forests are much better than the ones in Savannah and Old Ebenezer. If more people wish to move here to Ebenezer and the pine woods are not made usable, I would not know how to point out to one single person a piece of land upon which oak and walnut trees grow (that type of land they call good here). Hence the people would have to disperse quite far to their spiritual and bodily harm. On the other hand, they would settle that much nearer together if they accomplished something in the pine forest; for which nothing is needed but making fertilizer. In the forest they can clear four acres of bushes and trees sooner than one in another spot for planting, for the trees stand far apart and the grass and the feeble bushes standing between can be cut out with a scythe.

Saturday, the 25th of June. This afternoon God caused us to see and hear His great power and majesty once more. He caused the most violent thunder, with one lightning bolt after the other. The wind raged most violently, and tore roofs off and fences down; and with it there were the most violent bursts of rain, penetrating even into the stoutest houses. Nonetheless all occurred without harm (to Him be praise and glory for it in eternity), except that, as said, a few roofs were torn off, a few fences broken, and some trees damaged and thrown down. The rain was a benefaction for the land; but thereby God threatened us in those clouds, how much He could punish us if we abuse His benefac-

tions. It is just a year since we heard the sad news that the Spaniards had descended on the land. Pastor Muhlenberg has sent us
the 91st Psalm, from which we are drawing fairly good use.

Monday, the 27th of June. At this time we are enjoying from
our vineyard next to our house our first cultured grapes, and to
be sure both kinds, white and red. Because for some weeks I
have been unable to have the wild, superfluous wood broken
back, it has grown very long on the old vinestocks and has gotten
seeds and young, small grapes again. We saw that ripe, large,
white berries had grown on one rather low vinestock; and
higher up a young grapevine had also grown, whose berries
were like little peas. They will first ripen in a few weeks, so that,
if one knew how to handle the grapevine properly, one would
get grapes twice a year from a few vinestocks. The vintner on
General Oglethorpe's estate also found this to be proven two
years ago.

This year in our place we have so many peaches that people do
not know how to use them all. They would like to distill spirits
from them, if only we were provided with a few stills. The one
that we have in the congregation serves only a few families. To be
sure for some years we have dried peaches in the sun and in the
ovens like dried fruit in Germany, but they do not want to keep
here, rather they quickly get worms. On two of the trees in my
garden we have many apples, which, as I have seen in the Lord
Trustee's gardens, would grow very abundantly here in the
country if only people would take the proper interest in them. I
have no servant, neither does my dear colleague, and because
each and every householder has his own calling, we have to leave
lying many a task in our gardens.

Tuesday, the 28th of June. It seems peculiar to me that now
when the plot between Ortmann and Stephens is coming out,[22]
we have the story of Adonijah, who also plotted and conspired
with some people, contrary to good order and government.
This, however, cost him and his co-conspirators quite dearly, although he was a king's son. When Col. Stephens' son was at our
place in October of 1741 to draw our people into his plot, we
contemplated the story of the rebellious Absolom in regular
order.

Wednesday, the 29th of June. Yesterday evening the unmarried woman from Purysburg died, who some time ago had been taken into the care of our house for orphans and widows with her sick mother and two brothers. We saw to it that she lacked neither medication nor other necessary care, but it did not want to succeed. She had already been ruined fundamentally in Purysburg by a local doctor, a patch em up, and by other home remedies and very poor diet. The mother and the two brothers are almost in the same state. Whether the good that we spoke and prayed with her had a proper introduction to a penitent recognition of her misery and to a comprehension of Christ in faith, we cannot say with certainty. Such people are partly blind to the recognition of the basic truths of the Christian religion, partly they have absorbed many prejudices against our office. Hence it remains difficult to break through to them.

After the burial, I visited Mrs. N. She has a great feeling of her inborn and self-effected misery and talks quite freely, even in the presence of other people, with the recognition of her sins, especially against the sixth commandment. She also wishes for us to make known to the entire congregation her sins and infamies because she believes no sinner is as great as she, hence she is worthy to be looked upon with all shame. She complains bitterly at the frivolousness of her heart by which she has already lost much of God's grace that had already been presented to her previously. Her husband has a good preacher in her, and he is causing God's spirit also to act in himself. Young Lackner was present at the discussion and prayer, which we hope will also give him a good impression, especially as he likewise has a very good example in his wife.

Thursday, the 30th of June. Yesterday evening I received via Savannah a letter from our dear Mr. Jones, in which he reports the regular receipt of the letter I had written to him. At the same time he informed us in secret that General Oglethorpe has received permission from his Majesty the King of England to return shortly to London because of his private affairs, where he will not forget to advance our colony's interests that lie right close to his heart. He requests our humble prayer of intercession.

J U L Y

Tuesday, the 5th of July. Prior to the edification hour on the plantations I received a letter from Mr. Jonathan Bryan in Carolina,[1] at the close of which he informs us that thirteen Negroes were baptized by them on the 4th Sunday after Trinity and that still more were on hand who shortly are to partake of this great benefaction. He asks that we help them pray that these black persons might worthily turn to the doctrine of Christ that they profess. He is full of the praise of God for His great kindness that he manifests to them spiritually and physically and requests that we praise God with him and give voice to the 23rd Psalm.

Thursday, the 7th of July. Mrs. Schwartzwälder was bitten by a snake a short time ago and was in peril; but, because remedies were hastily used, she is now almost sound again. I told her what God was seeking with her, according to Luke 13:7–9, by means of His patience and forbearance, to wit, her true conversion, and that she become a fruitful tree instead of a rotten, barren one, otherwise it would be said: "Cut it down; why cumbereth it the ground?" With that I explained to her the verse: "Strive to enter in at the strait gate," etc. Over the door of her hut were inscribed in clear letters: "Strive so that thy zeal will glow, and may the first love draw thee from the whole world. Half love is of no account."[2] She is still very ignorant but displays little diligence to be saved from it. People such as that are commonly already satisfied if only they know that Christ died for them, taking comfort in His merit. Thus they hope to become blessed by indifferently using the means of salvation without true conversion.

Young Mrs. N. told me with joy and praise of God that last Tuesday she was quite awakened at the Zion Church by the Old Testament story, but she was also assured by His word on that same day that all her sins would be forgiven by means of her faith in Christ. Her husband, too, is now beginning to recognize that his Christianity is worthless and that he has made not the slightest start at it. She is now working on him from her own living experience.

Mrs. N. apologized in tears to me for her angry and ungrateful behavior; and she acknowledged that, at the instigation of her brother-in-law who has moved to H, she had sinned greatly against our ministerial office. To her he praised a Christianity that was quite easy and accommodating to the flesh; and he disparaged all the people in our place as bad people and would not recognize a single one as a true Christian or place a Christian trust in him. He participated in church and Holy Communion only for show. He dealt with me deceptively and insidiously, and thereby, indeed, he betrayed what a poor basis of Christianity was in him, although in the manner of many of these people he thought himself superior to others with his judgments. If another person had encountered in his marriage such extraordinary cases of misfortune, unheard of amongst us, as he encountered twice, one after the other, Mrs. N. would rapidly make her carping comments about it, as if such a thing happened because people were opposed to them, etc. I would wish that hereby his and his wife's insidiousness and falsehoods would dawn upon them, and also their great ingratitude against the many spiritual and physical favors we enjoy here.

Friday, the 8th of July. It is no longer a secret that Brigadier General Oglethorpe, with leave of the King, is going back to London, hence I must not keep it hidden any longer from our congregation, rather I explained to them what the reasons were, to wit, personally to respond to his enemies and malicious accusers and to advance the payment of the bills of exchange that were sent back. In the meantime the King is well satisfied with his behavior in his important post; and, as reward for his bravery, he has bestowed on him the rank of brigadier general. I also recounted to the parishioners, from the letter that we recently received from Mr. Jones, that the General had this colony especially at heart and that he was hoping vigorously to advance its interests and also to accomplish something good, for which he desires the help of our sincere prayers. Besides that reason, we have also to pray for this one: that such a gentleman is going away from this land, a gentleman whose name has been awe-inspiring even to the enemy; and it is not a good sign that he is traveling so long away from us. The inhabitants have surely deserved with their ingratitude God's real punishments this year, after His showing rod and sword a year ago from a distance. But we should step into the the breach by means of a penitent and faithful prayer and make ourselves into a rampart against the judgments we deserve. It is necessary to make these changes known to our parishioners so that they will not believe all kinds of gossip and will take to serious prayer rather than to arguments and discussion.

Our current story is of Nathan, whom God used as a guardian, benefactor, and profitable instrument against the Jewish race, of which we have here, in v. 11 ff., very important historical circumstances. This gave me a good opportunity to demonstrate to our parishioners the benefactions that God manifests to us by such instruments in our place in our time, as well as our Christian duty. With the beautiful words of verse 12: "So come now; I shall give thee counsel, so that thou shalt save thy and thy son's soul," we were reminded of the great benefaction of the Lord that till now He has imparted to us by means of the counsel of grace of our blessedness in all sermons and prayer hours; but the least have done it as did Bathsheba, who did not simply listen to Him but set to work and thereby accomplished much for herself and others. The people still accept a good piece of advice in physical circumstances, but very seldom in spiritual ones, which is a very clear sign that they love their bodies and the world more than their souls and heaven.

At this point we came to Proverbs 1, and the last part of this chapter was read aloud with some applications at the close of the hour in the Zion and Jerusalem churches. The last words also were indeed very critical to us: "But who hearkeneth unto me shall dwell safely and shall be quiet from fear of evil," etc., which words harmonize beautifully with our previous text at the memorial and thanksgiving celebration, Isaiah 1:19–20: "If ye be willing and obedient, ye shall eat the good of the land: But if ye refuse and rebel, ye shall be devoured with the sword, for the mouth of the Lord hath spoken it."

Saturday, the 9th of July. This entire week we have had rain and thunderstorms all day, afternoon, and towards evening; and yesterday the lightning bolts and thunder crashes were very severe. In Savannah it struck a couple of times and also smashed the flagstaff on the guardhouse where the banner customarily hangs on holidays, but we do not hear that any persons were harmed. The German people have not had a good beginning this year on their new land on the White Bluff,[3] for their livestock is still going bad because of contageous fever, and because their corn stands so poorly and they have little hope for a harvest, various ones of them are again laboring for daily wages.[4]

Mrs. N.[5] weeps and laments over her sins, and God seems to be using the double case of death of her children to awaken her from her sleep of sin and death. This morning she attested to me that she was often excited by the word and was awakened to penitence but her frivolousness stopped it so that she never caused it to come to the proper seriousness, and her unfaithfulness towards the tokens of grace and denigration of the word of God oppressed her greatly. Her husband was also talking with me yesterday on her account so that I might know in advance how things stood with her. To be sure, God has manifested much good to his soul, especially since his last illness; and he seems by some experience to have come to the proper essence of Christianity. Nonetheless he is still too rough towards his wife, as far as I can tell. Hence I wish that God might bless the treasured words of Collossians 3;12–13, which shall be posited tomorrow as the basis for our edification with the gospel for the Sixth Sunday after Trinity in him and others abundantly, so that things would come to the proper spiritual climate in everyone's Christianity and in the practice of their blessed duties and not always remain a piece of patchwork.

Monday, the 11th of July. I visited Carl Flerl's and Thomas Bacher's families this morning and was myself so abundantly edified by prayer and conversation that I can indeed truthfully call it an edification. We assuredly experienced what is written in Acts 9: "In the comfort of the Holy Ghost, they were multiplied." When I was in Bacher's house some time ago and examined a few texts of holy scripture in friendly conversation, I had just such heavenly pleasure; and, just as today, I traveled home with praise of God.

Tuesday, the 12th of July. This morning Mrs. N. told me that she had come into great anxiety and distress on account of her sins; she said her spirit was so low that she could not describe it to anyone. But God, she said, had blessed and looked upon her continuing prayer with grace and had presented her with the assurance of His grace last Sunday. She now further desired counsel from God's word so that she might be advanced in good ways.

I told her I would have to structure my counsel according to her acknowledgement and that I did not want to doubt that her claim was the truth, which would soon become manifest. She should, I said, sincerely and humbly glorify God in Christ for the grace she had received but simultaneously implore Him, zealously and constantly, to open her eyes more and more through the Holy Spirit, and she should also recognize as sins those things that in previous times she had regarded, if not as virtues, nonetheless as innocent things. The Old Adam was still strong in her, I said, and it would still cost much to crucify and lay him aside with all his members. I told her that it might come about that God would send her many sorts of things unpleasant for the flesh in order to test her, when it will become apparent whether the old or the new man holds sway, with the adversities and other occurrences befalling her. She would, I told her, have to be exterminated in her individuality and peculiarity and experience what poverty of spirit was. I had hardly finished talking when her old being reappeared in droves, as she began justifying herself, complaining about others, and opining that she could not be more scorned and destroyed than had already happened to her in Ebenezer. Therein she had a clear example that much about her was sin, but she did not recognize it as such and therefore her claim had little basis. She said that she was once again quite devastated, for she had thought to receive pure comfort from me but it was not fitting for the old Adam.

Wednesday, the 13th of July. Last evening I received from the manager Kalcher the sad news that the orphanage's herdsman said that his serving girl had told him that she had spotted the same sickness in his own cows that was raging a few years ago in Carolina and in this province and which from time to time is still taking away many cattle, to the great detriment of the poor. This distressed me and brought me to sighs and down upon my knees, at which the words from Psalm 90 were very impressive: "Who knoweth the power of thine anger? Even according to thy fear, so is thy wrath. So teach us to number our days, that we may apply our hearts to wisdom. Return, O Lord, how long? and let it repent thee concerning thy servants."

Thursday, the 14th of July. Today I wrote the pious Jonathan Bryan, who in his last letter gave me the joyful news that the first of some Negroes who had converted to God had been baptized on the 4th Sunday after Trinity. We fairly rejoice over this increase in the kingdom of God and praise the Lord with him. I informed him with a few words what good news we had received in the last Continuations (to wit, the 49th and 50th) from India, concerning the work of conversion of so many previously benighted and superstitious heathens, and I sent him a copper engraving of the dear instrument of the Lord, Pastor Aaron, which had been sent to us the other day.[6]

Theobald Kieffer's wife and her mother, the widow of Matthias Bacher, are in a fine spiritual state; and it was a great pleasure for me to talk and pray with them in their dwelling. Through His word God is disclosing to them more and more their previous sins, false Christianity, and selfmade comfort;[7] and He wishes to draw them into the valid righteousness of Christ, naked and unadorned. They regard very highly the grace that God has placed in young Kieffer and consider themselves quite unworthy of the benefaction of being so closely connected with him.

Young Mrs. Kieffer complained to me that a very great fear of thunderstorms and lightning has appeared in her; and she requested instruction on how to behave properly. I told her that God uses all kinds of means to search through the conscience and the hiding places of the heart and to draw the hidden thing into the light so that the sinner will humble himself beneath His powerful hand, and therefore, I said, this fear too would have to redound to her benefit. We say: "As we judge ourselves, so shall we not be judged." She should also cause herself to drive this distress into her prayer and there struggle so that she too might be able to say: "So truly as God is in Heaven above, so truly am I his beloved child, free from sin, entirely holy and full of grace. He wishes to be my Father, encloses me in His providence; protects me from misfortune, pain, and harm."[8]

Even if she prayed during inclement weather she should not believe that her prayer was displeasing to God because it took place in distress and anxiety, for He says expressly: "Call upon me in the day of trouble," etc. She might also sing such hymns as befit such circumstances, of which I mentioned several to her. If this fear nonetheless did not wish to die down, I said, she would have to be satisfied and believe that God found such chastisement necessary and would have to consider at the same time the example of Paul, who also implored the Lord three times to take away temptation but received the answer: "My grace is sufficient for thee: for my strength is made perfect in weakness."

Friday, the 15th of July. So many of the peaches are becoming ripe everywhere that one could load great wagons full of them. The people are profiting from them as well as they can, although many must spoil.

Our construction people had all the men from the congregation who were suited to work called to the mill to bring into the water and quickly to fortify a long wall of thick wood that they previously had made ready on land. By means of this wall we hope to be in a position to mill even with low water and even to set up a couple of rice stamps. With this wall and the dam a waterway is being made to let the remaining water through and the boats that go back and forth. In addition the canal through which the water is being channeled has now been improved considerably. It cost much labor, to be sure, but the people were happy to attempt it, and they will still turn to the labor of filling up the space between the wall and the dam with bundles of sticks and earth, because they are full of expectation that afterwards they will be able to be relieved of the communal labor.

This time every householder worked three days gratis, and they still might come every two days. But the carpenters, who have worked now constantly for fourteen days straight, have to be paid for their labor. We have something for that in the till, and our dear Lord will attend to the remainder, for He knows that the mill is indispensable to us. Whereas the river water is usually quite warm in the summer, today it was so cold that they could not stand working in it for long, rather they had to change around. This could take place quite well because we had enough laborers.

Sunday, the 17th of July. In the regular Bible story that is being examined from I Kings 1 in the prayer hours stands the

beautiful expression: " . . . the eyes of all Israel are upon thee
. . . " (v. 20), at which we remembered the 20th chapter of 2
Chronicles, our text a year ago at our day of repentance and
thanksgiving, especially the 12th verse: " . . . neither know we
what to do: but our eyes are upon thee," cf. Psalm 123:2, "until
that He have mercy upon us." At that time the distress caused by
the Spaniards drove us to prayer, and for the sake of Christ our
prayers were heard. Should we now doubt a gracious hearing
when the sickness in our cattle is really becoming conspicuous, if
we continue in faithful prayer? Indeed, we have in holy scripture the most glorious and most assured promises; we wish to
hold them out to the heavenly Father in this present distress in
humility and faith, as did Bathsheba in the current story, v. 17,
and await His hearing in quiet and patience according to His
will. We must recognize that we deserved a great judgment, yet
our dear Lord still only chastises us in small things, and with
mercy.

Monday, the 18th of July. Schwartzwälder has been ill and
near death for some weeks; and I heard recently already from
my dear colleague that God had begun a good work in his soul,
which I also found to be so today. He must have felt indeed what
a hideous thing sin is when it awakens in one's conscience, and
he will not forget his whole life long what anxiety and pain he
sensed in his conscience because of his sins. The distress taught
him to pray from the heart without his merely tying himself to a
book; and he is now working quite zealously on a poor, blind,
and unconverted person who promised also to follow him. Zübli
is his neighbor, who joins with him and his family in prayer and
examiniation of the divine word.[9]

Tuesday, the 19th of July. I visited our miller, D.E. /David
Eischberger/ and his wife, last week, and I found that our Lord
Jesus was carrying on the good work that He had begun in her.
Among other things she gave me to recognize the current condition of her conscience with the words from the hymn: *Hier
komme ich, mein Hirte! mich dürstet nach dir*, etc. She does not regret
our dear Lord's having led her out of Germany. She had recently
said, when letters were arriving and nothing came for her, that
even if she received nothing, she was still not sorry, for she re-

cognized that her leaving her fatherland redounded to her salvation. She is also working diligently on her husband.

Wednesday, the 20th of July. During the afternoon I talked with a person[10] who is naturally honest and simple but who has experienced nothing of true conversion, hence she also says that no sins oppress her, etc. I showed her from the above-mentioned verse how miserable things appear with the natural man, which, I said, she would have to recognize if she were to be helped.

Yesterday morning the Lord ordained that I receive the opportunity to talk with a person who in her own opinion is always doing penance. She holds up the verse from Apostles 26:18, but thinks that Satan has no power over her. I showed her, however, that it could be found in the verse that things appeared thus in all natural people,[11] and therefore she would have to have her eyes opened so that she would learn to recognize her wretchedness, otherwise she would never seriously seek to escape from it. Oh, may the Lord have pity on her!

Thursday, the 21st of July. Some of the German people in Savannah have collected money for the construction of the church of our dear Pastor Muhlenberg, whom they love and regard highly, in Pennsylvania.[12] I have received part of it and will receive part of it. In our congregation, too, our miraculous God placed a blessing on Pastor Muhlenberg's last letter such that many, without my doing or anyone else's, have done their bit from which by and by over 9 Pounds Sterling accumulated. In addition God did not scorn the collection amongst His people. I know that here and in Savannah they came from right righteous hearts and entailed many sighs and prayers.

Of a woman named Stricker (who, because of her husband carries a great cross) I was told by another pious woman that she, Stricker, disclosed to her that she now thanked God sincerely for bringing her to this country, for He had opened her eyes here to recognize her misery and Christ her Savior; otherwise, she said, she would have been lost in her blindness and wickedness. Now, she said, she was quite content with God's guidance when before she had been agitated and discontented. Two other women stayed after the prayer hour and attested to the mercy that God was performing in their souls. And I heard the same from two or more men. Praise God! For me it is now such a pleasure to proclaim the word of God in Savannah that I cannot express it. It is my intention in the future, God willing, to abide somewhat longer in Savannah so that I can visit the honest souls, which they consider something important.

Saturday, the 23rd of July. I am amazed that people in Germany have told, written, and printed that the 4th transport came to a miserable end on the sea, for after the captain and sailors died and no one was there to run the ship, the people of the 4th transport had to die of hunger and thirst and had to eat the flesh of one another. From this, one can see what the enemies of Ebenezer would like, and would like to have heard; but God did not give them that pleasure. In this regard I thought of the words of the 112th Psalm, v. 10: "The wicked shall see it, and be grieved; he shall gnash with his teeth, and melt away: the desire of the wicked shall perish."

Not long ago when examining the story and the beautiful words: "The eyes of all Israel look upon thee," we profited in our current trial (in which unfortunately the sickness is breaking out amongst our cattle) with the 123rd Psalm, where it says: "Our eyes wait upon the Lord our God, until that He have mercy upon us!" Thereupon is stated: "Have mercy upon us, O lord, have mercy upon us: for we are exceedingly filled with contempt. Our soul is exceedingly filled with the scorning of those that are at ease." His misery and this last matter of the behavior of the enemies towards him are what David, in prayer, cited as an argument to move the heavenly Father favorably to hear his prayer. And, since we have many enemies and secret enviers also in this country who would happily grant us the current punishment from which we have long been spared, this will also serve to our benefit and move our merciful father all the sooner to a favorable hearing of our prayer.

Monday, the 25th of July. Last week our two boats brought back forty bushels of salt and other things from Savannah. However, they were unable to come to the mill, rather they had to unload at another plantation because the water in the mill stream had dropped lower than it has been in the last two years. Sometime ago it was alleged that up in the mountains another river might have broken into the Savannah River, but this was only a guess without foundation, for now the river is as low as we have seen it till now. Our people are happy that they have the hope of using their good land beyond the mill stream, with this low water. It is extremely fitted for rice, grass, and hay; but for that reason we cannot plant corn, beans, and pumpkins because the bears, stags, and other animals have their proper lodging on this island and unless constant watch is kept all night and the alarm is sounded they will gobble up crops like that. Our people now have the most favorable weather for making hay, for it has been dry weather day after day.

Rieser's eldest son had me come to him and acknowledged sadly on his sick bed that it caused him regret and pain that till now he had rejected God's grace so often, spoken untruths, cozened me, offended his parents by disobedience and other means, etc. He had often made good resolutions in church, he said; he wished as soon as he came home to bend his knee and become a true Christian through God's grace but he always caused himself to hold back again. He deserved, he said, God's rejecting him; but he was requesting and hoping that God would still carry him until he had righteously converted, which was also the sincere intention of his heart. He admitted that God wanted him to be blessed and for that reason God had led him out from Salzburg with his family and had pursued him with His kindness for so long, etc. I told him among other things the verse: "Blessed are they that mourn," etc; and I introduced him to the story of the Passion so that he would learn to recognize what sin is and how severely God punished it in His son, like green wood. How would it turn out with those who remained dry wood?

Tuesday, the 26th of July. Scheraus received a very fine letter from a Christian bookbinder in Ulm. In it he finds the desire of his brother to move here to Ebenezer if the opportunity presents itself. Although this Scheraus is a weak beginner and is experiencing many weaknesses in the management of his plantation (as things are accustomed to go in this deficient world and pilgrimage), he nonetheless wishes to have his brother here because he knows that he would be pleased with our circumstances. May our merciful God nonetheless spare the poor with the sickness amongst their few cattle, for the sake of Christ, as most of their nutrition comes from them. Several times the verse occurred to me: "If the poor man crieth unto me, I shall hear him: for I am merciful." That is God's title of honor; "to help when the need is greatest," it says in the hymn: *Gib dich zufrieden und sey stille,* etc. We must look upon it as not by chance that in the Sunday Bible readings, before and after the sermons last Sunday, we began the Book of Job, in which the last chapter was compared with the first two, where we find that Job was stripped, as it were, of all his goods but afterwards our omnipotent and kindly God gave everything back to him abundantly.

Wednesday, the 27th of July. Young Mrs. N. of the 4th transport became violently sick Sunday and wished to have had me at her side, but I learned of it too late. For this reason I visited her this morning on her plantation that lies quite far off. A short time ago God brought her to the experience of His paternal love in Christ and assured her of the forgiveness of her sins. Now, however, He is picking her out especially from the people even more firmly to base the work that He has begun in her. She is also becoming a right faithful bride and disciple of the Lord Jesus, humbles herself beneath His cross, and is very well content with His guidance. The feeling of sin becomes very great in her from time to time; and just as she was full of the comfort of Christ's merit in her wordly respectability and fleshly assuredness, so now sometimes all her comfort wishes to vanish completely when she feels her past and present sins.[13]

It occurred to her in these days that if she were to die in this condition she would go to hell. I showed her, however, that a penitent and believing person, with every feeling of his misery, nonetheless has grace and the forgiveness of sins and that at and after justification the feeling of sin does not cease completely; rather, justification causes sins not to be counted against us. On the contrary, we are clothed with the meritorious righteousness of the son of God, and then the Father sees nothing damnable in us, although the flesh, according to Romans 8:1, is still there and causes all kinds of malicious agitations; but they are crucified and exterminated by the power we receive from Christ. During our conversation we came to the beautiful hymn: *Schwing dich auf zu deinem Gott,* etc., from which I read aloud to her some very important verses. Since her conversion she has been very close to Mrs. N., and their love for one another is right edifying. She shows herself to be active and righteous in good and evil days.

Friday, the 29th of July. My dear colleague, Mr. Boltzius, traveled this morning to Savannah; may the Lord teach him to cast out the net of the gospel so that he may make a great haul. May the Lord also aid and support me, poor person, so that both minister and parishioners may appear with joy before His countenance on that day. I visited Mrs. N. in the orphanage and spoke of one thing and another with her for her salvation. I showed her how one would know whether one had faith or not, to wit, if for example it could be said: "Lord Jesus, be my treasure, reconciler, Lord, and shield, and lead me as thou wilt, I am thine as I am, take me as thine own."[14] She could well remember these words, for she had sung the same ones last Sunday, and afterwards in the sermon she had learned them again. She had to acknowledge that things were thus in her case.

In the afternoon I visited old Rieser's eldest son and found him still in good circumstances. He was not there when I came; but when he walked into the room, he gave me his hand to indicate that I was a welcome guest for him. I was happy about that, indeed all the more so because for me it was something unwonted from him. I told him how it would have to be if one's Christianity were to become easy for one, to wit, from the very beginning one would have to surrender himself to his Savior so that, cost what it may, everything would have to be honestly ventured. I asked him what his intention was then. He replied that his intention was to attempt it seriously. Thereupon I told him he would get many enemies[15] who would seek to hinder him in it, but Jesus was the one who breaks through, He would blaze the trail. The only thing to say was: "Struggle rightly when God's mercy draws and converts thee so that thy spirit will be freed of the burden that weighs upon it."[16]

Saturday, the 30th of July. Gottfried Christ has been ill again for a few days. He had me visit him this morning, where a great many things were discussed with him, especially how to awaken him to a proper sincerity in his Christianity. He wants it, and yet he does not want it properly. He said that he thought of the prodigal son (Luke 15) and how he was reformed; whereupon I showed him that he not only made up his mind to go to his father but actually did so. In this he also demonstrated sincerity.

After one o'clock some people came to my chambers for prayer. In our current distress we are reading the 9th chapter of Daniel; and following his example we, too, humbled ourselves before the Lord and acknowledged to him our sins and those of the congregation. Our dear Lord indeed intends well in the current trial. He would like to separate the faithless heart from everything and draw it entirely to Himself. He has spared us long enough, for the sickness has been in the country for two years already.[17] But since we have not wished to notice it, He has finally had to come to us Himself. May He give grace so that each and every person may kiss the hand that strikes and chastises him.

Sunday, the 31st of July. In today's gospel (the 9th Sunday after Trinity) it says to keep accounts in one's household. I showed the parishioners that it will be said especially on that day, as well to me as to them. "For we must all appear before the judgment seat of Christ," etc. There no one would be able to slip through, as it indeed happened, I said, before men, as it is to be seen also in the gospel in the unrighteous householder who slipped through, to the harm of his master. So that we might be able some day to stand the test with joy, we encouraged ourselves, from Ezekiel 3:17–19, for each and every person faithfully to perceive his office and standing as a householder. May the Lord still help, so that it may be said to every single one of the ministers and parishioners: "Well done, thou good and faithful servant," etc.

Hans Flerl told me he nearly always wishes to weep but did not know why; yet I noticed from his talk that he longed greatly for heaven and wished soon to be at Jesus' side. Simultaneously it appeared so miraculous to him that, although he was still so dismal, he will nevertheless be found amongst other righteous and chosen ones. In the prayer hour I read aloud something of the 50th Continuation of the East Indian reports, especially the noteworthy example of John and the two persons who came to such an edifying end.[18]

AUGUST

Monday, the 1st of August. To be sure, I (Boltzius) had a some-what uncomfortable trip to Savannah, for it rained almost all day; yet I arrived home hale and hearty by boat at 6 o'clock with my traveling companions. Because Holy Communion was to be held on Sunday, the confessors came in from their plantations on Saturday afternoon and I spoke with some of them privately; and towards evening I held with others a preparation for Holy Communion about the first verse of the song *Welch' ein Sorg und Furcht soll nicht, etc.* During the evening prayer hour on both Saturday and Sunday we continued with our contemplation of the said important hymn; and we presented to the people both their great danger and the way to be saved from it. God granted us much edification in this.

On Sunday God again touched some souls mightily during both sermons on Ephesisans 5:15-17, as we could recognize from many circumstances, especially from their tears and confessions. The blessed Arndt's book of true Christianity is very useful again and again; and God has begun to lay much blessing especially upon the reading of the little book *Dogma of the Beginning of Christian Life.*[1]

A man who was a Roman Catholic soldier in France for many years and led a scandalous life in Savannah has converted righteously to God; and he took communion yesterday with people of our confession for the first time. Some are now beginning to confess to God on their knees the pains in their hearts. Nevertheless, it is still difficult for some; but the booklet *Dogma of the Beginning of Christian Life* will do them good service, especially in regard to the practice of prayer.

Tuesday, the 2nd of August. We are suffering many tribulations in the orphanage because of the cattle disease and other things, and the manager Kalcher is being especially hard pressed. God has given him strength to bear something; and, since God is loyal, He will not lay too much upon us and will refresh us during and after our tribulations. We sigh, "Return, O Lord, to us again and be merciful unto thy servants, O satisfy us early with thy Mercy, etc." During this pilgrimage our heavenly Father has, for our good, already let us come often into tribulation and hardship, but He has never let us remain stuck in them. Rather He has revealed his glory to us here as there at the marriage in Cana. This must strengthen our faith and trust and quiet and pacify our hearts before Him in all need, lack, and distress.

Thursday, the 4th of August. A great favor would be done to us if, for our own use, we could acquire a general land map by Mr. Homann or some other good author, likewise Pastor Schmid's *Biblischer Medicus*.[2] We are also asked whether or not we have any Schauer's Balm left over, because we find it of great value.[3] It also serves me very well in major weaknesses.

Dr. Francke has also asked in several letters what has been useful or not among the things that have been sent over. We can use everything that pertains to clothing, no matter what it is called. Also the buckles, combs, ribbons, yarn, etc. are also very much cherished. Most of the seeds have not wished to sprout because they were too long underway and presumably smothered. In the last chest we received a certain special kind of grain, which is to be sown as a trial in both the spring and fall. We are also maintaining a correspondence with Pastor Muhlenberg, through whose care we are hoping to receive such seeds as will grow in this climate. The seeds from there are said to do better in this country than those from Europe.

To be sure, we have received a quantity of kohlrabi, head cabbage, and chard from the European seed (such things and other garden vegetables grow very well in manured gardens); but it has never wished to produce seeds, rather it spoils before winter comes. However, this spring Mrs. Kalcher has (I don't know how) made the chard bear some seed, which, we hope, will turn out better than foreign seed because it was grown here. Otherwise, the plants in this country generally bear more seeds than in Europe. We have not been able to devote ourselves much to experiments because the householders and their families have had to occupy themselves with earning bread and food stuffs according to their external professions. We two, however, have lacked time and people for undertaking such things.

This year I have noticed that the orphanage's wheat has much larger kernels and more meal than that of other people; as a result the manager has received more and better meal than others in the community. This, in my humble opinion, comes in part from the fact that Kalcher cultivates his field with a plow and has sown on land that has already been planted and rendered mild and, as it were, tame soil, whereas the others have been getting along with the hoe. The rye, barley, and oats are as beautiful as in Europe and bear abundantly. I have seen barley that was sent here as seed whose ears this summer were as thick and full of kernels as I remember ever having seen in Germany. The most beautiful pot-barley could be made of it. All sorts of good could be accomplished at the orphanage as an example for the people if only we had helpers and means.

Friday, the 5th of August. Many people have already been supplied with brood mares, which they use primarily for breeding but also for drayage, plowing, and riding; and thus one horse must serve them for all purposes until they gain more resources. Here in this land one cannot get any horse-harness, which must be brought here from Charleston; and this is questionable if one cannot pick it out oneself. If Mr. Jones had not lent us a couple of horse collars with accoutrements, which actually belong to the storehouse, we could not have arranged any real drayage for the church, mill, and bridge construction. If some horse collars (since broad leather straps across the chest are not so serviceable) could be sent to us from London with some captain traveling to Frederica, we would be glad to pay for them. Our inhabitants wish to apply themselves gradually, with God's blessing, to more haulage in plowing and so forth than formerly in order to lighten their way of life.

We hope to get some plowshares from Charleston or Pennsylvania through Mr. Vigera.[4] He has also been asked to help our people to get some stills from there. If they had had them this year they would have been able to make proper use of their many peaches. Meanwhile, for distilling brandy from their peaches they have used the still that was sent to Mr. Zwiffler for distilling already in Old Ebenezer by the praiseworthy Society; and for that they give Mr. Thilo a small share of the brandy, which he occasionally needs as medicine.[5]

At this time I remember the green linen which we need for

curtains in the Jerusalem church. We hold the prayer hours here in the evenings; and, because we must leave the windows open in the warm weather, the air or wind blows on the lights, and this could be prevented by curtains. This is not to mention that the sun disturbs us in summer. With the fourth transport Senior Riesch[6] sent us a piece of glazed linen, from which curtains were made for four windows in the Zion Church, where there are still no glass windows. We are anxiously awaiting the sack cloth that is mentioned in the specification of the things found in the Halle chests, because we have had to get along right badly for some time for lack of them.[7]

Sunday, the 7th of August. This evening in the public prayer hour we especially commended Mr. Vigera's impending journey to our merciful God in the name of Jesus Christ; and we have wished him all good from the fullness of Christ as repayment for the love he has shown the fourth transport, the orphanage, and others. We have also made a covenant among ourselves before the Lord to struggle so that some time all of us here who have learned to know one another through the providence of God will come together in the Church Triumphant. I accompanied him to Savannah, where I had to give our letter packet to Col. Stephens and arrange some other things there for the German people. May God further our undertaking to His glory and our salvation and common edification, for which He will have occasion during the prayer hours with the German people.

Our people have also written some letters that are enclosed. They usually bring them to me unsealed, in which they have a good purpose; but I recently learned from a letter written by N. from N. that not very much good is concluded from their letters that are sent open. I have no commission to seal them; as a favor to me they should not be brought open to me for sealing, for I seldom have the time to read through them even though the people request it with good reason. I notice from miswritten points that many people in Germany are very suspicious; and this makes us, as far as possible, all the more cautious.[8]

Tuesday, the 9th of August. Last week I learned from Hans Flerl that he is very fond of the extract from Luther's *House and Church Postille Concerning the Gospel*[9] that was given to him at the last distribution, for in it he find so many splendid things that he must believe that Christ and His entire merits are with him. I recently sent Mrs. Kalcher the fifth volume of these extracts so that she might read in them what the blessed man writes concerning the verse: "Behold the Lamb of God, which taketh away the sin of the world." This explanation greatly edified her because she found in it, among other things, that we are no longer the bearers of sin, but rather the Lamb of God, which has carried all sins away.

Wednesday, the 10th of August. In the first house I visited, the wife was sick. Among other things she was very contented and satisfied with God's dispensation that He has now taken from her three head of cattle through the cattle disease.[10] She had had nothing, she said, when they arrived here; therefore it would be easy for Him to grant them some more now. They were not faring as they had done in Salzburg. There they had had to pay heavy taxes and sell their year's flax crop in order to pay what the authorities demanded. They had had three cows, she said, and they had had to sell one for the same reason. None of that was necessary here.

From here I went to the orphanage and visited Matthias Kurtz, who had also been sick for a while but could now go about some. I asked him whether or not he would like to be freed of his sins. "Alas," he said, "the sooner the better." Sin was no joy for him, he said, but a burden. Therefore I admonished him to come to Jesus, for then He would call him with the words, "Come unto me, all ye who labor and are heavy burdened, and I will give you rest." He said he had known the verse for a long time but had never really profited from it as much as now that he had received instruction.

Thursday, the 11th of August. Various important matters required me (Boltzius) to go to Savannah last Monday, among which the most important were to accompany Mr. Vigera and thus attest my love and respect in my and our congregation's name, to baptize a child, and to visit the German people on their plantations. All this took place, and I was greatly edified and blessed. After 8 o'clock this morning I returned hale and hearty to Ebenezer. The German people collected some 4 £ Sterling which they have dedicated to church construction in Philadelphia under the direction of Pastor Muhlenberg. This was occasioned by his last letter here. Most of them could give only a little bit, yet the total amounts to a good deal; and, because it was done by most with honest reasons and cordial wishes, God will be able to bless this little mite. He has great love among some of the German people. The name of the donor of each gift is written down, which will perhaps please their compatriots, friends, and relatives who may be there.

The German people have already done a lot of work this year on their new land (they are going to call the city they are to build Vernonburg because it is to be built on the Vernon River) and will get more corn and other crops than they expected a short time ago. They have very good land, and they will be able to situate their town very advantageously. Their plantations are laid out like ours so that neighbors can assist one another with fence making and in other ways.[11] The souls who received God's word were very pleased at my visit and would have shown me very much love, if only I had accepted it. But I had come only to serve them with my office through encouragement and prayer. They wished to hear something edifying from me and finally assembled in a hut, where we prayed together and took the most cordial leave from each other. The next time I hope to remain with them for a couple of days and to edify myself with them longer.

Friday, the 12th of August. As long as we have no hired hands, we cannot run a plantation seriously and thus advance the support of the orphanage and the good of the whole community and other people. Although Kalcher, with his three boys and the sickly servant Herzog, makes an extreme effort to plant as much corn and beans as is necessary for the household all year, that cannot be achieved, for a great deal is required for the whole year. Perhaps our dear God will give counsel so that the orphanage can be supplied with workers. Meanwhile we hope He will always let some charities flow from His good treasure to the support of these little institutions. May he make us grateful for previous benefactions, then that will be fulfilled in us: "Whoso offereth praise, etc." and "That is the way that I show him my salvation."

Sunday, the 14th of August. Today we again have had a cool day that was very comfortable for divine services. This whole summer has had more cool than hot days, and it has therefore been quite bearable and pleasant. Also I heard in Savannah that this summer has been better than in any former period. When such things are written to Europe, the people must form opinions about this climate as we formerly had. After our previous experiences we still feel that this land is not too hot. Rather the summer heat is of such a nature that it is very easy to bear and industrious workers can tend to their trades unhindered in summer as in all seasons, except that in summer from about noon to two or three o'clock they do their work in their houses or huts.

If it were so unbearably hot, how could my dear colleague and I make out, we who must ride back home very often at noon or one o'clock from the edification hour or other official duties on the plantations? Such heat, God be praised, has not hurt our health, even if we have talked ourselves tired before the ride. Also, on Tuesdays and Fridays our parishioners go a considerable way at noon back and forth to and from the edification hour. In the summer we usually have cool west or north wind, which tempers the air even at the hottest noon hour. In these dog days the nights have been not only cool but also fresh. We mention these and other apparently insignificant things in our diaries because we have learned from experience that rather amazing reports about this land and climate are running around, to which our friends will lend all the less credence when they read what we have observed.

Wednesday, the 17th of August. Some Christian friends in N. have sent Mr. Vigera a painting, which he has left behind in remembrance and which is now hanging in my study. This painting represents the ocean voyage of the fourth transport. The ship is sailing under full sail on the raging sea; but the eye of God is looking upon it, and it is being drawn from east to west by a rope held in the hand of God which is seen coming from the bright clouds. On both the place from which the ship has departed and on the place where it should go, that is, in Europe and America, four men are kneeling with hands raised to God; and it has the appearance that some of them are helping to pull the ship and the others to push it. Both are being done through hearty, humble, and communal prayer. Next to the hand protruding from the clouds are the words "Mine eyes are upon them which fear me." From the mouths of those praying come the words 1) "Renew me, O eternal light., etc." 2) "May the soul of Christ bless me, etc." 3) Praised be the Lord, etc." 4) "Lord God, we praise thee, etc." 5) "Praised be thou, Jesus Christ, etc." 6) "Thou thrice great God, etc." 7) "Lord Jesus, sun of grace, etc." 8) "To thee alone, Lord Jesus Christ."

The entire painting is very neatly done on canvas, it is two feet long and one and a half high and set in a gilded and well wrought frame so that it looks very beautiful and well decorates my study. If we did not have certain second thoughts, we would install it in the church as a reminder of our fortunately ended voyages, on which God has led us very marvelously with the rope of His love. Mr. Vigera once told us that the worthy Court Chaplain Ziegenhagen was inclined to give our church a costly, large painting which is to represent the Last Supper clearly and edifyingly. No one could rightly take offence at such paintings and Bible passages if our church were decorated with them. If our church could be painted some time both outside and inside with oil paint, it would serve not only for a decoration but also for longer duration. Such paint is not to be had in this country, we would have to have it brought from Charleston, and we are afraid we might be cheated.

Monday, the 20th of August. The great planters may look on it sourly that foodstuffs have become so inexpensive because of the well turned out harvest, but we look upon it as evidence of God's kindness to us. He chastises us with the cattle fever but otherwise grants so much of the treasures of the earth that even the poorest can get along. The cattle fever is still spreading about and has not only done great damage to the town cattle, and is still doing it daily, but is also beginning among the cattle that are grazing on the good pasturage between the plantations and Abercorn; and on Saturday several head of cattle were found dead in one spot. The cattle that come home every evening to the plantations, God be praised, have been spared so far by this dangerous disease, except that Eischberger, who lives in the midst of it all, has lost a cow from it. Otherwise we have noticed nothing.

Wednesday, the 24th of August. I had a very refreshing hour this afternoon in the orphanage. I came there just as Kalcher and some other honest souls from the orphanage were beginning to pray. N. has been very ill-disposed for some time toward N. and N. However, as in the case of Lydia, God has opened her heart and brought her to a recognition of her great error and to divine sorrow. Before the prayer I made an effort to convince her of her corruption and of what mercy the Lord was now again beginning to show to her soul. I also gave her and N. instructions to flow together rightly, from which all those in the orphanage would have great profit. If only I could get a pious single person whom I could engage as a supervisor for the children, it would be most useful to me. We lack the means to take on someone as an overseer, and God must first grant the means. During the prayer I was exceedingly blessed by the words of Jesus: "All power is given unto me in heaven and in earth. Lo, I am with you always," and I trust that the Savior who hath been raised to the right hand of God will apply his power to our salvation and good.

Thursday, the 25th of August. Today the surveyor general, Capt. Avery, finished his work here so that he can render the council in Savannah and the Trustees a conscientious report about our land and the great work of our inhabitants. I see it as a divine dispensation that this man came to us. Since for the most part we have land that cannot be made productive except by manure, while our cattle near town have been largely destroyed by the cattle fever, perhaps the Lord Trustees will let themselves be moved to lend a hand to our industrious workers, who would gladly nourish themselves in an honorable way. God makes use of many means and ways to do good to His people, and He will surely know how to bring something good out of this.

This surveyor has offered to survey for us a large piece of land of several thousand acres, which, however, lies some twenty-four miles from our place. This land, which is highly praised by him and others, lies on this side of the Ogeechee River, which is a well situated navigable stream, where in time the capital of this land is to be situated.[12] There is said to be a harbor there already made by nature more beautiful than any other in America so that the largest warships can anchor there; and it is advantageously situated for trade or for war with the Spaniards or French. The land intended for us does not lie in the same area but further upstream; and the surveyor is making such proposals, namely, that in time others of our compatriots who wish to come to our community from Germany would settle there so that they and we would hold in common the great fir forest between the Savannah and the Ogeechee Rivers for cattle-raising and other uses.

If a straight path to there were laid out and made, our place and the new place would be no more than eighteen or twenty English miles apart, which one could ride in five hours. Avery makes the further proposal that, if more people in other transports were expected, some of our old inhabitants could take possession there and be useful to the newcomers through their experience. It stands with God whether anything can come of that and whether these suggestions are feasible. We wish to await the time and not toss the matter to the winds. This man himself will examine the land more closely; if he finds it according to his and our wish, he will report it to me so that I can view it with some of our people.

Monday, the 29th of August. In this summer God has mercifully spared us from instances of death in the community, and our fevers have been quite bearable. To be sure, some are complaining of fever, but they can tend to their business as soon as the paroxysms are over.

Tuesday, the 30th of August. It is a sharp tribulation for us that our cattle are being taken away from us. May Jesus, to whom all power has been given in heaven and in earth and who bears all things through His mighty word, have mercy upon us and our little children, who need the milk most for their nourishment, otherwise the poor people in this strange land lack nourishing things.

Today I spoke from God's word with the sick woman from Purysburg who has been cared for with her two sons for several months in the orphanage, and I spoke especially about the verse:"Teach us to remember that we must die."[13] and I showed her that it was a wise thing to prepare oneself through penitence and faith for blessed eternity, and then I prayed with her. She wept a great deal and attested that she regretted her sins; but I well noted from her lamentations that she was lamenting her physical circumstances, and I was even more strengthened in this belief by a story. There are now twenty-one people, large and small, in the orphanage, which is not very large. With this woman and her two sons twenty-four are there. Toward Sunday, Christian people come in from the plantations and lodge in the orphanage. Now that God has taken our cattle, milk, and butter, the food is not so rich as previously, yet it is prepared as well as possible for the sick. As much as God gives us, we gladly give back, thoughtful of the verse: "It is better to give than to receive." But we must have patience until our Father grants us more. The reading lesson Philippians 4:11-12 fits a few people.

Wednesday, the 31st of August. This morning I was occupied with distributing the late Klocker's small legacy, which Hans Flerl has been keeping until now, among his three children. Among other things we remembered the verse Jonah 2:9: "They who cling to their vanities (as is accustomed to happen in the division of legacies) forsake their own mercy."[14]

SEPTEMBER

Thursday, the 1st of September. Among the physical benefactions that God has shown my and my dear colleague's families we rightfully count the well water which is found in our courtyard near the house. We have such abundant water both in winter and in summer that the neighbors can be supplied with it, too; and it has a very pure, fresh, and healthy taste.

Monday, the 5th of September. High praise be to God, who has deigned to allow me, poor man, to complete the first chapter of the First Book of Kings in today's evening prayer hour and has so greatly strengthened me in body and spirit from beginning to end in the presentation of this very important mystery-filled Bible story that I could often feel right noticeably the influence of His goodness and the assistance of His spirit in this procedure, to my and our parishioners' edification.

I have never realized that so many delightful things pertaining unconstrainedly to Christ and the nature of His kingdom are to be found in the stories of the Old Testament. During our prayer, meditation, and re-reading, He reveals one thing after another in accordance with His unmerited kindness. In this regard I often think of the passage "Seek, or search in scripture . . . it is that which beareth witness of me," namely, not only the prophetic but also the historical books. May He make us grateful from our hearts for the incomparably costly gold of the gospel, which we, so to speak, have found in large veins in this holy mine and which has been revealed to us in the said first chapter for our rich edification.

We have always been able to inculcate impressively the Order of Salvation that stands there in conversion and rebirth. What Solomon said to the supplicating rebel Adonijah at the conclusion of this chapter is what Christ says to each and every sinner: "If he will shew himself a worthy man, there shall not an hair of him fall to the earth (bygones will all be forgotten and forgiven, and I shall receive him into my grace and protection): but if wickedness shall be found in him, he shall die," etc.

Tuesday, the 6th of September. Matthias Kurtz, the Salzburger whom Court Chaplain Ziegenhagen helped come here from Cadzand, has been very well provided for so far in the orphanage. He and his wife have had very much physical weakness and would have gotten on very badly if he had received a plantation immediately. He and his family have now been in the orphanage for almost a year, and now they are insisting zealously on having a plantation. Young /Martin/ Lackner will become a helper to Kalcher in the orphanage, and he is sellling his plantation and crop to this Kurtz for a fair price. It is situated a good distance below the mill and is very inconvenient with regard to church and school; but the Salzburger Kurtz disregards all this. His three little girls, who are now studying, we wish to retain among the orphans; but he wishes to take them along. He is poor and has a frail body, and she is in the same condition. As a beginning the orphanage is giving him two pounds Sterling cash, two hundred pounds of beef, and ten bushels of corn.

Wednesday, the 7th of September. A German painter[1] in Charleston /Jeremias Theus/ has completed in duplicate in our church the gospel verse: "Rejoice greatly, O daughter of Zion: shout O daughter of Jerusalem: behold, thy King cometh unto thee: he is just and having salvation." Mr. Vigera offered to pay him, but he wishes to donate this work to our church.

Thursday, the 8th of September. Last Tuesday Mr. Causton[2] brought us the news that General Oglethorpe will make every effort possible to prevent the introduction of Negroes because he knows better than any man in this country or in London it would cause great harm and danger. He intends to carry out the Lord Trustees' design of having a large party of English and German hired hands brought into the country by whom the land can be occupied and the inhabitants can be helped. Their plans aim at having the serving men and women sent over here at the cost of the Lord Trustees. They would have to serve for five years and would receive four pounds Sterling annually as wages. From that they would receive two pounds for themselves for buying clothes, while two pounds would be paid back to the Trustees towards their passage money, which would amount to ten pounds in five years. From this (because a passage amounts to about six pounds) they would and should have a surplus if some servants died underway or in this country or if perhaps a householder were not in a position to pay the wages for his servants.

No householder would be able to hire his servant for more than one year; afterwards the servants could hire themselves out to other householders for a year, as is customary in England and Germany. In this way the Lord Trustees could benefit the householders who hired such servants by giving them a bounty of two shillings on every bushel of crops for the first year, one shilling for the second, and sixpence for the the third, etc.; and thus they would lend them a hand and put them in a position to carry on their farming with their own work force. However, it would be done differently with entire families; the householder would settle them on their lands and supply them during the first year with provisions, tools, and cattle. Then each year they would receive the half of all crops and cattle as a repayment of their expenses [3]. These propositions pleased our inhabitants; and they have requested three entire families, thirty-six hired hands, and three maids under the above bounty conditions. For otherwise no one would be able to pay an annual wage of four pounds. We must wait to see whether so many single servants can be sent here.[4]

The people from the upper plantations on the Savannah and Mill Rivers have been occupied for several days in constructing a good and broad way for driving, riding, or walking and in building bridges and causeways over the swampy places so that they can go back and forth without getting wet. Formerly we have had to make a detour on horseback if we wished to go from the town to some plantations. On Sunday mornings, or whenever they wished to go in or out in bad weather, they have wet their shoes and clothes, and by this they have harmed their health. This will all be more convenient now. If we had the means, we would like to repay them for this necessary and useful work. I would have liked to do that for a long time, but we could not presume upon them because of their much other work until they encouraged one another to do it. Thus God gives one thing after another.

Friday, the 9th of September. A person with whom I spoke remembered once again what good Mr. N. did for her and her family; and she wishes to write to him and give him especial thanks. On this occasion she also mentioned her departure from Salzburg. She said she had had to suffer much underway. They often tried to take her children away from her, but the Lord had always prevented it. On the way they met a drayman who was heading for Augsburg. This pleased them very much and they went along with him in their wagon. When they came to Munich they crossed a long narrow bridge. When they came up to the gate, the drayman was let in, but the gate was shut to them. Because the bridge was very narrow, the man had to unharness his horse and push the wagon back over the bridge from behind, whereupon they were greatly laughed at. Afterwards they rode around the city and caught up with the drayman again at the other side of the city, which gave them much pleasure.

Finally they reached Augsburg, where people were greatly pleased at their arrival and took loving care of their reception. This was something very sweet after the rough treatment in Salzburg and on the way. May the Lord be a rich Rewarder of all the good that was shown to this family, both then in Augsburg and later in Memmingen. Once they were in great poverty, but then the Lord sent them through Mr. N. a bowl of flour and two pounds of rendered butter, which stood them in very good stead. They often suffered want, but it was never so great as at that time. Thus, the Lord knoweth how to provide for His people when the need is the greatest and to awaken someone who will send them something even if he does not know of the present great lack. This is indeed true: "Oh God! Thou art today so rich as thou hast been in eternity."[5] This contradicts the unbeliever when he says that God no longer shows himself as formerly; for I truly believe that He shows himself today as He used to do. He who believes will say,"My trust is entirely in Thee, strengthen me in my soul, then I shall have enough here and in eternity."[6]

Sunday, the 11th of September. Praise be to God who hath strengthened poor me in these days to preach His gospel. For our today's gospel for the 15th Sunday after Trinity we had as an exordium: "Doubtless thou art our father . . . thy name is from everlasting." We heard from both the exordium and from the gospel how glorious it is to have God as your Father. Such people are very blessed and can be comforted in all difficult circumstances of body and soul. If one is a believer, then his belief can be powerfully strengthened by circumstances that are presented very simply in the gospel by the best Schoolmaster, our Lord Jesus. Otherwise it merely remains something literal which one can comprehend a bit with his reason but which will not hold water.

Among other things, we heard from the exordium and its last words, "Thy name is from everlasting," that the believers had profited already at that time from everything that God had done for His children in early days. Thus they did not do, as many unfortunately do nowadays in Christendom. When the ancient miracles of God are related, they say, "Now God does no more miracles." Unbelieving nominal Christians speak thus; but true Christians do not say this but show that they believe in the God who wrought miracles in olden days. All those who can not yet call God their Father were admonished to struggle first of all, as Jesus Christ says: "But seek ye first the kingdom of God, and his righteousness." May our dear Father strengthen His children in their faith so that their hearts will always be open and so that He will be able to enter into them more and more. And may He also teach them at the same time to follow their trade loyally and to let our heavenly Father take care as to how He will keep them. In conclusion we sang, "Act like a child and lay thee in thy Father's arm. Ask Him and beg Him until He has mercy on thee, as is His custom. Then, after a well fought struggle, He will bring thee through His spirit out of all cares on ways that thou dost not yet know."[7] Isaiah 64:5 says, "And yet we were helped." We, too, will learn this in our present time of hard tribulations caused by the cattle sickness.

Wednesday, the 14th of September. Now that Leitner has properly established himself, our congregation is provided with a good smithy. He burns his charcoal on his own plantation, even though he had never learned to; and now that I have helped him get inexpensive iron in Charleston, I hope he can give his services cheaper than in Savannah; and then he will have no lack of work. As he told me, he had a skillful master in Augsburg. However, he regrets that he was not more industrious during his apprenticeship; yet he did learn enough to give our community good service with his trade. His stepson /Peter/ Arnsdorf is learning blacksmithing from him. He is a skillful inventive type, and with time he will be able to do his stepfather good service. In addition to this smithy we also have two locksmiths in the community, who have set up their shops. One of them is Brückner and the other is Schrempf, who has bought all his tools from his stepfather Lackner[8] at a fair price and under certain conditions. If they will plant something for their own needs so that they will not have to buy everything, then they will get along quite well.

We are lacking carpenters and board-cutters, therefore we must postpone from one time to another many things that should be built. Cultivation with just a hoe costs the people so much time and effort that it can hardly be described. Therefore, as long as they do not advance seriously toward getting plows and perhaps getting hired hands, they will scarcely be able to run their own farms and with their money serve their neighbors who employ workers and day laborers and let them earn money.

Thursday, the 15th of September. At the request of Col. Stephens we have written down the names of all our inhabitants, both large and small. In Ebenezer there are now 81 men, 70 wives, 6 widows, 52 boys, 59 girls, and 11 serving girls, and thus 279 souls in all. Jesus has redeemed them all with His blood. May He make them all obedient to the gospel! He wishes, alas, that we all wished it!

Friday, the 16th of September. Mr. Meyer's house was so far prepared last week that he could move in last Tuesday. As soon as I can get some sawyers I will have the house boarded all around, as has been done with the orphanage. Otherwise the beams into which the shingles of the four walls are fitted would rot very quickly because of the rain that penetrates them.[9] This house has a heated room, a bedroom, a hall between the heated room and the bedroom from one door to the other[10], and also a good attic over the heated room and the bedroom. The roof is as well protected with good cypress shingles as the church is. A good durable staircase leads to the attic. Near the house is a fine fenced-in courtyard with two gates, one giving to the street to the church and one to the orphanage yard. The kitchen stands on a convenient spot behind the house so that one can step with three steps from the back door of the house to the kitchen door[11]. To one side along the fence is a hut in which wood, barrels, or what you will can be stored dry. In the heated room there is a brand new iron stove, which is heated from outside; and therefore we do not have to worry about any discomfort from smoke in the house[12].

In the heated room and the bedroom there are glass windows, which are something rare in this country. If we could get workers and if God would grant us money, a small cellar should be dug near the house, which Mr. Meyer greatly needs. No well is needed here because he can use the well at the orphanage, which is some thirty steps from his house. Mr. Meyer has sold his old house to the old /Theobald/ Kieffer, who with his family has made do until now in a very miserable hut. As an aid in his housekeeping Mr. Meyer will receive as much provisions as he needs each year; yet he himself will have to buy wheat, meal, butter, and molasses for brewing beer. A girl from the orphanage will serve him; and, because his wife is always sick, his laundry will be done in the orphanage. As a salary he will receive two pounds quarterly, and for that he will give his services to the orphanage and also hold a writing lesson in the school. I wish from my very heart to be useful to each and every person in the congregation and to lighten their burdensome lives as well as my own. One must resign oneself, however, to the will of God and be content with His guidance. For indeed we are not worthy of the least of His gifts; yet every day He doeth everything good for us.

Sunday, the 18th of September. If I had the means to provide the skillful carpenter Kogler and his wife and two children with a dwelling and livelihood near the orphanage, I would gladly do it for the sake of the community. It is too much for him to have to work hard from time to time as a carpenter but also tend to farming and cattle raising; and we well see that he will not be able to stand his all-too-great work very long. He himself hopes that it will become easier for him in the orphanage and that he would be able to help the community more with his work.

Monday, the 19th of September. Under the date 5 September the Charleston papers that Mr. Vigera sent me reported a dangerous throat disease is raging from time to time, by which many children have been carried away. Also, the last storm on 30 August is said to have done much damage to some ships and boats at Charleston and further out in the sea. Those are nothing but bells to penitence. If only we would all apply them to that purpose!

This morning I received the cards[13] or silk curries which came to Charleston in the chests and have been brought to Savannah. They are a gift from Mr. N. from N., our great and worthy benefactor; and we learn from letters he has recently sent to Mr. Vigera that this gentleman is gladly contributing all he can to advance the good of Ebenezer and especially of its silk manufacture. During my meditation today I was blessed by the verses Psalms 113:5–7. May the Savior, who has ascended to the the right hand of God, look with the eyes of His mercy upon those who allow so much good to flow from their wealth to our widows, orphans, and others.

Tuesday, the 20th of September. Mrs. Glaner has taken leave of the orphanage, in which she has been for so long as a patient; and she praises God for this physical and spiritual good which she has experienced there. To be sure, her hand is not yet entirely healed, but it has recovered enough for her to help her husband in little things and lighten his household and farming tasks, especially since he and others now have their hands full with harvesting corn and beans.

Friday, the 23rd of September. This morning Mrs. Graniwetter told me on the way to church that she and her husband are witnessing God's gracious blessing on their field this year, for they had all sorts of crops so abundantly that they could not re-

joice and marvel enough at such divine kindness. This afternoon I visited this pious family to see for myself this physical
blessing in the field and to praise with them the great and kind
Giver. I let them lead me through their entire field and was very
much pleased with the sight of the abundant corn, beans,
squash, sweet potatoes, peanuts, and turnips; and I was encouraged to the praise of God. They did well in planting between the
cornrows not only beans but also squash, which have grown very
large and can be harvested much more easily than the beans,
even if there are many of them, since they bear so abundantly
here. Graniwetter must build a new hut in order to use the old
dwelling as a barn for storing his crops.

From the last letter from Court Chaplain Ziegenhagen we
have learned that the deceased Duchess of Kendal in London
remembered our orphanage in her will, but the amount of the
legacy was not yet known to him.

In this country there is a kind of black wildcat that sprays water when a person or dog comes too close[14]. This causes an in-
credibly nasty stench and so penetrates one's clothes and the
horses and dogs that come to the spot that one can get sick from
it. This stench does not disappear in many days even if not the
least bit of the nasty water has been sprayed on anything. A few
days ago Leimberger had such an experience and had to put his
clothes, saddle, and bridle outside of his house and change all
his clothes; for otherwise he would have filled the entire house
with the unbearable stench he had brought back with him.
Once, when I was passing by the woods at Purysburg in a boat,
we could smell the stench of this disgraceful animal from far
away, which made us very sensitive.

Saturday, the 24th of September. Some men were busy this
week in preparing woodwork for the well at the orphanage,
which is worth preserving. The posts and boards in this very
beautiful well, which are exposed on all four sides from the bot-
tom to the top, are rotten. Therefore we are afraid it may col-
lapse if there is a heavy rain; and the repairs later would cost
more than if a new well were to be dug. If someone among us
could risk making bricks, then the first bricks should be bought
and used to wall up this well, which is entirely indispensable for
the orphanage and the neighborhood. Wood rots very quickly

here in this country. Meanwhile we must do what we can; and I am happy that some people have found time for preparing this woodwork.

Simon Rieser of the fourth tranport has long been an invalid because of a badly cured fever, and therefore he has not been able to work much in the field. Today he told me that, praise God, he is well again and that he has entirely lost the swelling in his feet. I reminded him of the beautiful words of Psalm 119: 71. "It is good for me that I have been afflicted; that I might learn thy statutes" (cf. Psalm 67).[15] We have much to learn from David in I Chronicles 29, who well applied the short time after his recovery. In his time he served the will of God, and that is the duty of all Christians according to I Peter 4:1-3. "For he that hath suffered in the flesh hath", etc. "That he no longer should live the rest of his time."

In presenting this point publicly, I have been able to refer to the consciences of very many of our parishioners as witnesses that in their sicknesses the first statement: "For he that hath suffered in the flesh hath ceased," etc. had hit the mark. Their hearty and sincere confession of this, their reconciliation with their neighbor, the restitution of unjust wealth, and other tests give clear evidence. However, the injunctions "should no longer live the rest of his time in the flesh," etc. and "not to live to the lusts of men," etc. have surely not been realized in all, rather they have again become frivolous and secure.[16] It is from such disloyalty that, although they use the means of salvation diligently and always learn, they still never come to a recognition of the truth and therefore do not experience what David confessed about himself. "It is good for me that I have been afflicted; that I might learn thy statutes," likewise,"Before I was afflicted I went astray."

Thus it stands with many among us: they go astray, they stick in prejudices, fall from one thing to another, come to no certainty of their state of grace and are thereby so distressed that they do not even rightly recognize their erring and misery. This will continue so long as they learn nothing right, so long as they do not labor and become heavy laden. For of them alone Jesus says in Matthew 11 that they should come to His school and learn gentleness and humility of heart. However, because God loves their souls, he bears them with the greatest patience, showers them with many benefactions, and also comes with His chastisements, as last year with the dreadful invasion of the Spaniards and in this year with the cattle disease, etc. Oh, if only He could achieve His purpose in us all with His words, benefactions, and chastisements as well as with our dear David, whose dear example and precious treasure of grace dwelling in his heart shine out to us very powerfully from our present Bible story in I Chronicales 29. The grace with God granted to him as a basis for his righteous nature He also wishes to grant others, yea, all of us, for He would gladly have many servants and children here in the struggling church and there in the Church Triumphant. In the New Testament the mercy of Christ no longer a future but rather a present and right abundant grace (I Peter 1:10).

Sunday, the 25th of September. On this 17th Sunday after Trinity at the beginning of the sermon we remembered the great blessing that our loving and merciful God granted us two years ago when he caused us the joy and satisfaction that we could consecrate our little church in town with the word of God and prayer; and in the past two years He has granted us a right rich opportunity to prepare ouselves for blessed eternity through His word, prayer, and trusting use of the holy sacraments. Whether everyone has applied this large part of his period of grace for this purpose was a question I presented the parishioners, who had assembled in a large number, for them to search in their consciences.

Not only in the times of the apostles, but even now in our days many souls have been converted to God through a single sermon and have thus been prepared for blessed eternity. It should therefore cause great embarrassment to all those of us who have not been righteously converted to God in the past two years (to say nothing of the previous badly applied period of grace). To the praise of God for the many spiritual blessings we have received in our little town church and elsewhere we sang the beautiful song: *Singt dem Herrn nah und fern,* and in the repetition hour we remembered the little verse that we had contemplated at the consecration: "We will rejoice in thy salvation, and in the name of our God we will set up our banners."

Thus hath our gracious God shown Himself even in the greatest need and is still showing Himself, and will continue to show Himself (as we can hope from His goodness in Christ). Thus we could repeat St. Paul's dear words in 2 Corinthians 1:10 to God's praise and the strengthening of our faith. If our little church is small and simple in comparison with other churches in Christendom, and if the people who assemble there for divine service and edification are poor, unimportant, and simple people, our great God does not scorn the small and simple, rather He loves it and dignifies it with His providence, protection, grace, and help, as we recognize from many places in the gospel and from the edifying passages in Psalms 113:5–7 which served as its basis.

Thursday, the 29th of September. Old Mrs. Bacher revealed to me with tears that she is now in preparation for Holy Communion and that she is faring this time as before, namely, that the old sins that she committed in Salzburg and in the Empire[17] were occurring to her again and causing disquiet and pain; and therefore she was very sorry that she could not break through and achieve rest. She was very afraid, she said, of sickness, death, and judgment. Because she had the characteristics of a penitent sinner, presented to her the feelings Jesus had for sick and miserable sinners; and (because she is in the preparation for Holy Communion) I made use of the hymn *Jesus Christus, unser Heyland, der von uns den Zorn Gottes wand.* Her daughter, the young Kieffer woman /Maria/ attested a contented heart at the words "It is finished," from which she had profited this morning. Because the old mother was grieved that she could remember so little from the sermons and edfication hour, I gave her instruction in this, too, and a few mnemonic aids for remembering what she had heard.

OCTOBER

Tuesday, the 4th of October. On some places on the plantations there are so many beans and peas that the householders and their families cannot collect them all. If a rain or heavy frost were to come over them they would all spoil. Therefore they are giving other people who have few or no beans permission to harvest as many as they wish for themselves. They do not all ripen at one time and cannot be mown like the peas but must be plucked.

Meanwhile, others are standing on the poles in full bloom, or the young beans are gradually ripening. It is a very beautiful, useful, and productive crop; only the harvesting causes the greatest trouble. Whoever has many children can accomplish something with them.

Wednesday, the 5th of October. If Kogler moved to the orphanage, we would assign some boys, especially from the orphanage, who would learn from him carpentry and mill construction and also cabinet making, in which he is the most skillful man among us. It is too bad that we have no pious and skilled handworkers in this country or at our place. To be sure, we have shoemakers and tailors, but still too few carpenters. We could also use a good cooper or barrelmaker. We have no tanner for red or white leather here, who would have enough work to do all year. We also lack a wheelwright. We have smiths and locksmiths, who also have enough work even though the community is small.

Thursday, the 6th of October. Old Mrs. R. called me to her sickbed and told me with tears that some old and previously forgotten sins had occured to her in her fever paroxysm and that her conscience was compelling her to confess them. One case had occurred in Salzburg and the other in the poorhouse in Augsburg [1]. The first was a sin of commission and the second a sin of omission. She is praying diligently to God that He may properly reveal to her her wicked heart and all her transgressions and grant her true penitence. What she is now experiencing is to be seen as a hearing of her prayer and at the same time as a sign of grace, for it costs our dear God much to bring sinners to penitent recognition of their sins.

Tuesday, the 11th of October. My dear colleague Mr. Boltzius caught a severe fever this afternoon. In the morning he had ridden out to the plantations to hold the edification hour in the church, where he found the sermon easy, but the ride to and fro difficult. Last Sunday he gave them the 103rd Psalm to read at home, in which, among other things, stands something that we wish to note in these circumstances through the aid of the Holy Ghost: "The Lord is gracious and full of compassion," etc.

Thursday, the 14th of October. This morning our boat came from Savannah and brought the two large chests that were sent to our little flock from Augsburg and Halle. The former departed on 1 Feb. and the latter in March of this year. Both arrived here in very good order, and nothing was spoiled in them. Oh, what a great blessing there is in books, medicines, and linen! It is very great, we are not worthy of the least of it, yet the Lord doeth so much for us. Oh, if only the Lord, through so many signs of His love, could draw all of us in Ebenezer to Himself and strengthen and keep us in His grace. May He help us in this. I call upon Him among other things in the name of Jesus Christ. May he let all of us in our houses and huts come to the point that in all of them there will be lovers of the Lord Jesus like Martha, Maria, and Lazarus, who were a beautiful cloverleaf of pious brethren of whom we heard this evening in the prayer hour. He is glad to be with such people, He comes to them gladly and brings Himself along with all His grace and blessing.

Now the Lord will help us to come together for ever with all dear benefactors whose hearts love Jesus alone and to love and praise eternally the Friend of our souls, our dear Lord Jesus Christ, for all the good that He has done for us and them. In our prayer hour we particularly requested for our dear benefactors that our dear Lord Jesus might raise His hands and bless them as we read in Luke 24:50-51. For, when He took His leave there from his dear disciples, He raised His hands and blessed them; and while blessing them He ascended into heaven, where He sits on the right hand of His dear Father and distributes nothing but blessings. Consequently, He will also hear our poor prayer for our worthy benefactors and do nothing more gladly than bless them. May He let them experience this whenever they might need it.

Tuesday, the 18th of October. In the past week I had an opportunity to speak with N. and her family; and I had to tell them that they should not just darn and patch on their Christianity and merely set a new rag here and there on their old heart. Their entire heart must be new, and the dear Lord Jesus will gladly grant it to them. That should be dear to them, so they should pray for it.

Friday, the 21st of October. In the name of my dear Lord Jesus Christ I (Boltzius) am beginning to enter into our journal some points about what the Lord is doing for us in spiritual and physical matters, now that our dear Physician, whom we must ever trust and love, has begun again to strengthen my poor frail body mightily. May He be humbly praised for the salutary chastisement I have experienced. I had deserved swords, and there were only rods, yea, little rods, with which He wished to correct me for my good. May He let me spend the remaining days of my life zealously in His service and for the good of my parishioners, just like the man of His own heart, our dear David after his recovery. Like St. Paul, may I forget what is past and reach forward for what is before us. Resolution and will are there; and, because He is Alpha and Omega, Beginner and Perfecter, He will also grant success. May He be heartily and humbly praised for having, according to His great mercy, right noticeably strengthened my dear colleague in his physical and mental powers and having granted him joy and blessing (of which I have evidence) in the performance of his office and also strength for keeping and copying our diary. May He repay him and all righteous parishioners for their zealous intercession for me.

To be sure, my double tertian fever has been dispelled already for several days through the constant use of medicines from Halle, but chiefly through the blessing of God. Beforehand and afterwards I have had rather good rest at night, yet my lassitude and physical weakness was so great yesterday noon that I was unable to undertake any work. Since yesterday afternoon my strength has been increasing gradually. Last night I gained still further strength through a healthy sleep in the midst of the charitable gifts in my room; and our dear heavenly Father right distinctly prepared me, my dear colleague, and others to hold the thanksgiving sermon for this day of the suffering and death of our dearest Savior, whom I always had in mind during the distribution. This was the thanksgiving sermon for the abundantly received harvest and for the spiritual and physical blessings received from Augsburg and Halle in the two chests. This, God be praised, was done to my and others' inner satisfaction and to the stregthening of our faith!

The linen, stockings, ticking, feather beds, black and green linen, crape, etc. which were to be distributed had been divided in past days and yesterday afternoon by me and my dear colleague in the presence of his and my wife and laid out very regularly. Of me this was true: "He giveth power to the faint; and to them that have no might he increaseth strength." And it is truly a dear benefaction to have a loyal colleague. Contrary to expectation, last Sunday in my solitude God let the verse Tobit 13:5 fall into my eyes and heart: "See what the Lord hath done for us! With fear and trembling praise him in his works, and laud him who ever reigneth." The godly and reverend Tobias encouraged his dear people to this, namely, to a living recognition of the goodness and benefactions of the Lord and to a hearty and humble gratitude for them; and to that all of us were publicly awakened and encouraged.

It has now been ten years since the Salzburgers of the first transport gathered in Augsburg to come here to America and since we in Halle received the call to come to them with much prayer and cordial wishes for blessing. When we now think back on what has happened among us since then on the journey and here in this country, where one transport after the other has come to the Ebenezer congregation, we may well call to one another: "See what the Lord hath done unto us!" This is true also in regard to the richly received harvest and to the beautiful damask church cloth that has been prepared for us and to the all the gifts that we have now received from Europe. We diligently remembered the gifts in the former chest, especially the beautiful books which were distributed at that time to us and the congregation; and we remembered that we had received a beautiful spiritual blessing from the hymn *Was gibst du denn, o meine Seele, Gott, der dir,* etc.

Afterwards the present books that were to be distributed among both young and old were named, and the proper use of this great and unmerited benefaction was praised to them. It was also a great thing, we said, that God had provided so abundantly not only through linen and books for the healthy but also through a large supply of sure and proved medicines for the sick and those who might become sick. It is truly written: "Knowest thou not that God's kindness is drawing thee (oh Ebenezer) to penitence" (not compelling thee through frightful things and judgments, but through benefaction as bonds of love)? Or, according to our saying: "See what the Lord hath done unto us!" and is still doing.

Finally we all knelt, praised our Father reconciled in Christ for all His kindness and benefactions shown to us and our benefactors and requested for them as a reward for their love all that He Himself recognizes as useful and salutary for them. After the blessing had been said we went to my house for the distribution, where 103 adults and 65 children of the second and third transports and a few others here in this country who had come to our community for the sake of God's word received, some of them linen, some of them ready-made shirts, some of them other things pertaining to clothing, *Treasure Chests*,[2] and other edifying little tractates.

The first and last transports had been supplied with linen the previous time, that is, on 8 June of the current year, and these people received the *Treasure Chest, The Glory and Dogma A.C*, the splendid little tractate of the conversion, some very important sermons, some Bibles, hymnbooks, and Arndt's books of True Christianity.[3] Some men who have until now done very good service in the community and have not demanded payment received something special from the gifts as repayment for their disinterested industry. This will serve them and others as an encouragement. The distribution took place in the most beautiful order and to our great pleasure; and I believe that most went home laden with a spiritual and physical blessing and in their own houses and huts will praise the Lord according to the instructions they have received for His goodness and allow their hearts to be filled with the living recognition of His goodness and benefactions as we saw in the case of the godly Tobias. For their mouths will flow over, and housefathers and housemothers will be, as it were, ministers and tools of God in their homes, which will greatly expand the kingdom of God among us. Hallelujah! Bless the Lord, o my soul, and forget not what good He hath done unto thee.

In Savannah we and our congregation always enjoy very much good from a German man Löwenberger and his wife,[4] and we cause them much disquiet both day and night in our lodgings. Therefore we are going to allow them something from this beautiful blessing from the crate in place of any repayment. We also gave some other honest Germans in Savannah some *Treasure Chests* that were sent here abundantly in the former and present crates for our general enjoyment. From them God sends much edification to both the sick and the whole. In Abercorn there is but one obliging Englishman with two sons, who always receives us both day and night when we come up from Savannah and entertains us as best he can in his great poverty. We gave him, too, a ready-made shirt, which he will surely consider a great benefaction, since I know how he has acted in the case of much simpler things we have given him.

A great benefaction has also been made through the Venetian theriac and the 50 vials of Schauer Balm, which the worthy Mr. Caspar Schauer has sent here as a gift and which has already served the needy when circumstances required.

Saturday, the 22nd of October. Toward noon I went to young /Jacob/ Kieffer's plantation as exercise and also to conduct some external business; yet God granted me a spiritual blessing in a short conversation with him and his wife. When I asked her how her heart had occupied itself this morning for her edification, she told me that she concerned herself with the important Bible story of the circumstances of Solomon's anointment, which we had contemplated publicly some time ago, especially that the people, both large and small, had shown themselves so joyful and merry at it as had also happened in the New Testament at the entry of Christ, the true Son of the daughter of Zion, into Jerusalem. Just as David's heart must have rejoiced deeply that everyone had received his dear Solomon with pleasure and joy of heart and were pleased with David's counsel and commands, it is our heavenly Father's earnest desire and most deepfelt pleasure when poor penitent sinners comfort themselves and rejoice in His Son as their Redeemer and Savior; and it is a shame that so few rightly understand the essence of Christianity. They put it all into mere legalistic practices, in omission of evil, and the exercise of good or at most into prayer; and they forget the most desirable thing, namely, the trusting acceptance, savoring, and seeing how loving the Lord is.

In a lovely hymn of the late Pastor Freylinghausen it says:"Moses no longer rules, Christ's free spirit leads us, captivity is over. Whoever belongs in God's house can now enjoy being His child through the penitence of Goel. Halleluja!"[5] I am deeply impressed whenever I perceive from the words and stories of my parishioners that the word I have preached has táken root in their hearts and is bearing good fruit. The Bible stories are, as it were, an excellent vehicle to teach and instill the most important truths into their souls and also an *adminiculum memoriae*[6] in order to remember the most important points again.

Sunday, the 23rd of October. This evening we came together in my study for the first time this fall to begin our song and prayer hour. The beginning was made with song and praise of God, then we learned the song that suited today's text: *So führst du denn recht selig, HErr, die Deinen.*

Sunday, the 30th of October. In today's gospel for the 22nd Sunday after Trinity I laid the important words of 2 Samuel 12:13, in which David's sincere confession and Nathan's gracious absolution stand close together, as a basis for my sermon and for the edification hour. Because, in the absence of my dear colleague, I had to present my meditations about them in both the morning and afternoon, I took the time to explain each and every point with the noticeable assistance of the Holy Ghost and to lay it on their consciences. A woman's conscience had become aroused; and following the afternoon sermon (which was also a catechisation) she came to my study and poured forth her troubled soul. She is already a blessed soul, and that which God with His light has granted her to recognize concerning her perdition and her deficient penitence and faith will serve her for much progress toward good.

Monday, the 31st of October. The manager Kalcher showed me an English letter that a widow from Frederica had written him to thank him for all the good that she had enjoyed from him and his wife at the time of the Spanish invasion; and she sent his wife a pound of coffee and some silk ribbons as a token of her gratitude. At that time, at the request of the minister Orton, a private hut was evacuated for her and her children next to the orphanage; and she may have also received some service from the orphanage, which she still recognizes with thanks.

NOVEMBER

Thursday, the 3rd of November. Until now the young locksmith Schrempf has been looking around in the community for a helpmeet and has finally proposed to Kieffer's fourth daughter;[1] and her parents have promised him their consent. Both old parents, the betrothed, and Pichler and his wife / Margaretha Kieffer / came to my study yesterday towards evening with the request that the engagement take place in my presence and be consecrated through the word of God and prayer. I first gave them some admonitions as to how they should conduct their marriage in a Christian way if they wished to be comforted with all proofs of divine blessing. Afterwards I read them the very lovely 61st chapter of Isaiah, from which I had refreshed myself and my family at our morning prayer hour. Here I had a rich opportunity to present to them the splendid treasures of the New Testament that our Lord Christ merited for us so bitterly and which He now grants so readily through the gospel to all the miserable and brokenhearted, to them that mourn in Zion, and to spiritual captives. It was an opportunity to ask them to concern themselves earnestly with these treasures and with the royal bridal jewels, as stands in vv. 1-3, 6-10. Finally, we knelt and requested from our merciful and loving God a manifold blessing for this engaged couple and other people.

Saturday the 5th of November. A woman from the plantations sold my family for two shillings one pound of cotton ready for spinning, which money she will use this evening to pay toward her shoes. She is very poor and has always gone barefoot until now and has always borrowed shoes from her sisters for a few hours to go to church. This so touched my heart that I gave her the remaining two shillings necessary to cover the cost of the shoes. She has an honest disposition.

Tuesday, the 8th of November. According to His great mercy, our dear God granted me a great blessing from the catechism. May He let me remain forever a student of the same! This time the 17th and 18th questions followed in regular order from the Questionnaire. Oh, how much lies in it! It is good for me that I have to preach one thing at various places and therefore frequently; thus our loving Savior grants me His blessing often. May He be praised for the catechism. Oh, how blind man is to have made so little of it in previous times. Now may He be praised for forgiving this, as He does everything; and may He grant me, and all others, both large and small, a fine spirit to make better use of it.

Friday, the 11th of November. This morning N. informed me that the Lord took his little child to Himself last night. He said his wife was requesting me to come to her before the edification hour. Therefore I rode to her and learned that in the past night she had been in a strange mood. It had seemed to her that death was seizing her as well as her child. Because she did not know that she could die saved, she felt such fear and trembling that she did not know what she should do. It would not have been possible to speak with my dear colleague or with me, so she had Mrs. Thomas Stocher come to her as a pious woman. [2] I told her that our dear God wished by that to make a new attempt and to see whether He could now win her completely. Until now, I said, she had often been forcefully awakened, but it had not yet come to a change of heart. Her heart was still malicious, it clung to both Jesus and the world; and therefore she should beg Him to make her hard heart both mellow and soft and draw it entirely to Him. The world should see that she is otherwise and no longer has her old mind. There was still grace for her, I said, and that is why our dear God had let her live, but it must become truth.

Tuesday, the 15th of November. After the edification hour I was called to M.K. /Matthias Kurtz/, who now dwells at the end of the plantations but was in the orphanage. I visited him because he had become weak since yesterday. He could now tell me with certainty that the Lord Jesus has forgiven him all his sins. He must trust Him in this now, he said; for, after all, one trusts even a man when he promises something. Soon thereafter I learned from his wife how he had come to that conclusion. To wit, last Sunday night he had become very miserable in his body, and then he saw at once what a miserable sinner he was, so that he became very frightened. In these same circumstances he was able to learn what he had not been able to believe before, namely, that a person could not die blessedly despite all his external good practices if he did not truly participate in the grace of God.

When the wife noticed this in her husband, she told him what he should do as she had heard it in the sermon: "Approach God, and He will approach you." When he did this, he also experienced it. Oh, a loyal God, who so gladly comes to poor sinners. Among other things I told him that it is written there concerning our Lord Jesus, "He will rejoice over thee with joy, he will rest in his love and will forgive thee, he will joy over thee with singing." If the Lord had forgiven him according to His loving kindness, then He would do him even more good according to his heart's desire and show him one mercy after the other. That should awaken him to strive toward Him with even greater hunger and thirst and thus apply the short remainder of his life well.

The old tailor M. /Metzger/, who is an old sinner, also summoned me in the evening because he had become very sick. I told him that our dear God meant well with this sickness. He wished to bring him into quietude and to a recognition and a feeling of his sins. Therefore he should run through his entire life from youth on, for there he would find many dreadful sins, with which he has caused his Savior so much sorrow and effort. It is better, I said, if the sinner allows himself to be brought to a recognition of his sins during his period of grace rather than have them all presented to him on the day of judgment. There will be no more mercy there, but here even the greatest sinner can achieve mercy if he will just let himself be brought to true penitence and conversion. Therefore he should ask our dear God for this. At my departure I told his wife that she should hurry, for it is better for a person to think of his salvation in healthy days. She did not know, I said, whether she would become sick. If she did, she would feel physical pains at that time.

Tuesday, the 22nd of November. After today's edification hour I spoke on the way home with a person who always wished to learn better to consort with the Lord Jesus in a childlike and trusting manner. In the previous week she had heard about that and had wished to hear about it again because she was greatly lacking in it. She is already with Jesus but allows herself to be drawn away from Him easily by the feeling of her frailties. Then she must begin all over, and thus she cannot progress further. In this regard I told her something of the love that she, as a mother, had for her children. If they did something wrong and felt sorry about it, what would her attitude be? She should reflect whether our Lord Jesus would act the way she would expect Him to be disposed toward her. This she could well understand. Therefore I said to her the words of Jesus: "Abide in my love."

In the afternoon another person came to me who wished to know definitely that she stood in well with Jesus. She had so many obstacles, she said, and could not reach Him. Therefore I told her how, through the power of Jesus Christ, she should seek to break through all the way to Jesus like that woman. In addition she should bring all her burden to Him and ask Him to do with her what he said in Matthew 11:28, "Come unto me all ye that labour and are heavy laden, and I will give you rest." Then she should remain still before Him so that He might do to her according to His heart's pleasure what he so gladly does to poor sinners. He washes them in his blood, rejoices over them, forgives them everything so that such souls gain strength through such attestations of love of the Lord Jesus to love Him in return.

Wednesday, the 23rd of November. I visited a couple of children who have been in the preparation hour until now. First I spoke to the parents alone. I asked about their divine services at home and asked whether the father prayed jointly with the mother and children. She answered that they were not yet doing so, he was too shy to do so and thought the children could do it better. But I encouraged him in this and promised him to send the little book that the late Professor /August Hermann/ Francke had published for the good of the Glaucha congregation[3].

Friday, the 25th of November. In the evening we buried the little English boy whom the schoolmaster Ortmann had taken in and who died this morning. At the interment I and others profited from the words that the Lord granted and that Pastor Muhlenberg called out to us in a letter: "Behold, the Bridegroom cometh!" If this is to be comforting to us in the future, then we must really love it now. For who should be afraid of conversion? The Bridegroom is indeed there, who demands only the "Yea" word and one's entire heart. He wishes to do it all Himself: wash us and purify us, confide in us with grace and mercy, give Himself entirely to us, and celebrate marriage with us in time and eternity.

Saturday, the 26th of November. I (Boltzius) surely have good grounds to praise our merciful God for the chastisements of sickness He has sent so far by which He has deigned to dignify me for my salvation. He has revealed to me all my sin and many of the spiritual trespasses which I have committed since childhood so vividly and has drawn me thereby to His throne of judgment that I have well learned to crawl to the cross of Jesus Christ and to the free and open Spring. In me, too, Jesus has made true His own words: "Him that cometh to me I will in no wise cast out," likewise, "Come unto me all ye that labour and are heavy laden, and I will give you rest." He has comforted me greatly through new assurances of His merciful forgiveness of all my sins and the gift of being a child of God and caused me to rejoice in my Christianity and my office. Now, among others, I dearly love the 34th Psalm, of which I made use during my journey to Savannah with all its dangers and which I made profitable to the other German people through the assistance of the Holy Ghost.

Sunday, the 27th of November. With this Sunday we began the new church year; and we must recognize, to the praise of God, that he has noticeably strengthened us in body and mind through the preaching of His word and that He has granted our souls much blessing, just as we have perceived this in some of our parishioners and hope to experience further. May Jesus transfigure Himself in our hearts through His spirit by means of the holy gospel through His entire merits so that, in this year, too, we can present Him and the whole abundance of his mercy to our dear parishioners and thus draw them to true conversion and godliness.

After the morning service I received the news that Matthias Kurtz had died this morning and (as we do not doubt) passed away in peace.

Monday, the 28th of November. This morning at eleven o'clock Matthias Kurtz was interred, and I took as the theme of my address in the churchyard the lovely song: *Allenthalben, wo ich gehe,* etc. For some time at all the burials of our dead I have begun to read a funeral hymn out of our hymnbook to the pallbearers in the cemetary and instructed them to understand it correctly and to apply it to their own salvation. Most beautiful and impressive funeral hymns would otherwise remain, as it were, a hidden treasure in the field, since such hymns are seldom sung publicly, and do us little good. With the above-mentioned hymn, which is

composed very edifyingly and at the same time clearly and simply, I profited in two places today while visiting my parishioners.
When there is a body to be buried on the plantations, it is
brought to the Zion Church and set down at the door. The minister goes into church with the people and we sing before the
body is carried away and a suitable chapter or psalm is read
aloud and everyone sings. In town the funeral party assembles
in the house where the body is; and the body is carried from
here to the cemetary after the singing, prayers, and reading of
the chapter.

Wednesday, the 30th of November. Some time ago, with the
approval of the community, the Salzburger Stichler[4] began to
establish a tavern in an orderly and Christian manner (not for
the harm, but for the use and convenience of his neighbors). For
this he recently received, in my presence and at my recommen-
dation, a written permission or *licentia*, which the English call
a "licence." In it is written his duty, namely, not to allow any dis-
order, gambling, or suchlikes and that he will appear at Easter
again before the council with two witnesses, from whose mouths
they wish to hear about his conduct. This license serves primarily to prevent any barroom from arising in that it forbids any
and every person at our place to sell or serve strong drinks to
guests. We greatly need an orderly host among us not only for
the sake of the local inhabitants but also for the sake of strangers,
for otherwise the people come to our houses as if they were tav-
erns and demand everything for money or gratis; and, if they
are refused, they grumble.

The two pious men, Hans Flerl and Theobald Kieffer, Jr.,
who are cutting boards for the orphanage, have hit upon a fine
invention to cut cypress boards, which grow in low areas where
the trees grow in great number. Here the land is full of water,
because most of the year all the places in which such trees grow
are flooded. Therefore they cannot dig a saw-pit for cutting
boards as is usual, upon which the wood that is to be sawed is
rolled and sawed by the man above and the man in the pit.
Therefore they have made four ladders upon which they can
saw the tree into boards up high. I am please that we are getting
cypress boards for covering the walls of the houses all around,

which boards last much longer in all kinds of weather than the boards of pine and fir,[5] as we have sufficiently experienced in the case of roof shingles.

DECEMBER

Friday, the 2nd of December. As I was riding to the edification hour on the plantations this morning, a pious Salzburger spoke to me through his fence and told me that the Lord had done great things in him at the end of the old and the beginning of the new church year and that he was right joyful in his faith and in his love for Jesus. Since yesterday he has had great refreshment from the pithy verse in Galatians 4:4, "When the fulness of the time was come, God sent forth his Son," etc. From it he had received much edification a year ago on the first Christmas day.

Tuesday, the 6th of December. During the day there was lovely sunshine; wherever it could penetrate, the snow and ice were melted, whereas they remained where it did not reach. On the way to the plantations some bushes hung so far down that one could not ride properly on the path. The snow must have bent them down. May our dear God grant us grace to contemplate better now how great He is in the realm of Nature. Because we see the snow so seldom, it appears so marvelous to us and we must be ashamed that we did not contemplate it in Germany.

Wednesday, the 7th of December. I spoke with a man about his condition. He said the Lord had already done much in him and had already awakened him often, but it had not come any further. I told him that our dear God had often held before him the sugar of His grace and had wished to lure him with it but that he had not wished to follow. It is written not only "Wake up, ye who sleep," but also "Arise from the dead." This last he should do. The Lord Jesus has enough power, I said, as He called to Lazarus in the tomb: "Lazarus, come out." Thus he calls to the spiritually dead, if only they wish to follow His call; and the Lord Jesus will loosen all bonds so that they will be free, and that means that, when that occurs, Jesus receives the sinners and eats with them.

Saturday, the 10th of December. Because there are no plowshares to be had here in this land or in Carolina and it is uncertain whether Mr. Vigera can send such things from New York and Pennsylvania, we would be glad to see a Christian friend in London, to whom our desire for such farm implements was made known, buy for us a few metal plates or unfinished plowshares with the necessary saws or blades. Each pair of neighbors would like to have a plow of their own.

Sunday, the 11th of December. The many catechism books that we received in a large book chest through the care of Court Chaplain Ziegenhagen have been fetched in large numbers by both adults and children especially in the last church year, since on Sundays, instead of the Sunday epistles, the catechism has been treated clearly and edifyingly through questions and answers. We detect a greater love and respect for this dear little book in many of our parishioners than we did in past years. For the old fantasy had set itself very firmly in many hearts that the catechism was only for children. Now very few of these catechism booklets are remaining. For our congregation, and for other Germans of our confession in the country, it would be a great benefaction if we could again receive a supply of such books.

Tuesday, the 13th of December. Among us there is a great desire for Christian servants of both sexes and all ages, of which a rather large number could be used. Our married couples are mostly young and have small children and therefore greatly need maids for the children and other household chores. The men would progress much better in farming and cattle-raising and accomplish more if they could get loyal hired hands for a fair wage. May God provide in this lack, too, and let us detect the footsteps of His providence.

Tuesday, the 20th of December. The young locksmith Schrempf is a skillful and industrious worker; and, because he can make all sorts of things, there is always enough work for him. It is a great obstacle in his profession that he can get no black sheet-iron in either Savannah or Charleston and that he is required to disassemble old hoes and pans and hammer the plate when he needs it. He would also make wind stoves at a cheap price for our people in their rooms if only he could get sheet metal; and this would be a great benefaction for many, especially for those who are sick or have small children. He has asked me to help him acquire a hundredweight of sheet metal from London, for which he will gladly pay. We do not like to burden our friends with such matters, since they have other important and complicated business; yet we also know that this will not displease them, rather, in accordance with the great affection which they bear for us, they have asked us to write them frankly about all the things we lack. Therefore, we have taken the liberty of allowing the lacks and the desires of our parishioners to flow into our diaries and into the letters to them.

Wednesday, the 21st of December. We have now transfered our singing lesson to the church. My heated study, in which we formerly held it, was always filled with people and with dense smoke and heavy vapor that was very uncomfortable for us in our singing lesson and prayers and especially for me afterwards, because I do my business in this study. We have enough room in the Jerusalem Church, also the windows and doors are protected so that it is tolerably warm even in cold weather. If anyone sings and prays with holy zeal, he sings and prays himself warm and disregards a little external discomfort for the sake of the great spiritual profit. This singing lesson is now held immediately after the regular prayer hour. For this purpose those people whose circumstances allow them to attend the singing lesson remain in the church. We sing for only a half an hour, then we pray so that not more than three quarters of an hour are spent. We keep it short because many still have chores in the evening or else have small children and would for that reason have to miss the prayer hour or the singing lesson if they lasted too long. Yesterday we learned the very important communion song: *Jesus Christus, unser Heyland, der von uns*, etc.

Sunday and Monday were the Christmas Celebration

In it God granted us not only mild weather and much rest and tranquility, but also rich edification from the grace-filled and comforting gospel of the incarnation and birth of our highly meritorious Savior. On the first day of Christmas the entire congregation was together in the Jerusalem Church in great numbers. In the morning we preached from the regular Christmas gospel and in the afternoon from the epistle reading in Titus 2; and we also held catechism. It was all directed toward helping both old and young to be able trustingly and actively to recognize our Jesus, who sold Himself dearly for us and came into the world and into flesh through incomprehensible and ineffable love. On the second day of Christmas the congregation was divided and the divine service was held simultaneously in the Jerusalem Church and the Zion Church as is usual on Sundays and feast days. The word of God was preached from the gospel of Luke 2:15 ff.; and it was repeated in the afternoon through questions and answers.

Wednesday, the 28th of December. After the death of her mother the young Kieffer woman /Anna Elisabetha Depp/ had her brother and sister come to our place, for which she, and especially her husband, Jacob Kieffer, had a good purpose. Her brother is an apprentice with the shoemaker Zettler and has gone until now to the preparation hour; and, because he is also diligent and attentive during the sermons and prayers, he has noticeably lost the blindness in spiritual matters that he brought here with him and has experienced the power of the word in his heart for a recognition of his self and his salvation in Christ. He took Holy Communion once in Orangeburg[1] but little understood what it meant and experienced even less with regard to penitence and faith. Now he longs for Holy Communion among us and will probably be admitted to it next time.

Friday, the 30th of December. Mrs. Schweighoffer has arisen again from her sickbed and has gone out again. She visited me in the afternoon and registered for Holy Communion and praised the grace and love of God that she had experienced on her sickbed. It now holds of her too: "I shall guard myself all my life long from such anguish of my soul." She was misled by her own heart which she trusted more than other people who had insight and experience. Formerly she could not be at all convinced of her obstinacy, inordinate love for her children, and suspicion against other pious people. Now Mr. N. has convinced her, changed her heart, and brought it to grace so that she rejoices, albeit with trembling.

Sunday, the 31st of December. N. /Ruprecht Steiner/ told me that in the last edification hour God had opened his wife's /Maria's/ eyes through His word so that she is beginning to recognize her blindness in spiritual matters and to be ashamed of her poor Christianity. He is working loyally on her; but he is also requesting me to visit her. She is ashamed to learn to read and to let us instruct her further in Christian dogma; and that is why her husband asked me for advice. The chief and basic truths of the Christian religion, which everyone must necessarily know to achieve salvation, are already known to this honest and diligent woman. However, because God has revealed her perdition to her, she considers herself blind in all things and wishes to continue with instruction in town if no other arrangements can be made for it.

I do not believe that this woman has to go to a special instruction lesson, if only she will diligently visit the sermons and edification hours as she has done so far, and carefully repeat with her husband what she has heard and pray zealously about it. Concerning the last two points she failed in previous times, and this was a cross for her husband. He is very much concerned with his Christianity. If the Holy Ghost can penetrate to him with its office of chastisement and persuasion, then it can also perform its instructive office in her and transfigure in her the divine truths that she hears and which she herself is gradually learning to read. Then she will find everything that is necessary for salvation to be clear and savory.

It is a pity that our Salzburgers cannot acquire any hired hands or maids and that all their work lies on their own necks. Most of them have small children and they are sometimes sick, and all this hinders them in many spiritual practices. God will also care for them more in this. This story by Steiner will serve me through God's grace to make better use of simplicity in my sermons and to repeat the matter preached all the more diligently.[2]

May our loving and gracious God be cordially and humbly praised for all His assistance that He has granted us in our office so abundantly in this year that has just ended.

Appendix I

HYMNS SUNG IN 1743

Hymns followed by F-T and volume and song (not page!) number are reproduced in Albert Friedrich Fischer—W. Tumpel, *Das deutsche evangelische Kirchenlied des 17. Jahrhunderts* (Gutersloh, 1916, reprinted Hildesheim 1964). Authors of all identified hymns are listed in (AF) Albert Friedrich Fischer, *Kirchenlieder-Lexikon* (Gotha, 1878, reprint Hildesheim 1967).

Ach Gott! du bist noch heut so reich, als du bist gewesen ewiglich . . . (Oh God, thou art still as powerful as thou hast been in eternity), anonymous. (See Joseph Th. Müller, *Hymnologisches Handbuch zum Gesangbuch der Brüdergemeinde,* Halle 1916). p. 103; Sept. note 5

Allenthalben, wo ich gehe . . . (Everywhere I go), by Ahasverus Fritzsch. F-T. p. 122

Auf, auf, weil der Tag erschienen . . . (Up, up, because the day has dawned), by J. A. Freylinghausen. p. 116; Oct., note 5

Du meiner Augen Licht . . . (Thou, light of mine eyes), by Johann Georg Kehl. p. 5

Du sagst, ich bin ein Christ . . . (You say I am a Christian), by Johann Adam Haslocher. p. 6

Erleucht' mich, Herr, mein Licht! . . . (Illuminate me, Lord, my Light), by Ernst Wilhelm Buchfelder. p. 6

Es kostet viel ein Christ zu sein . . . (It costs a lot to be a Christian), by Christian Friedrich Richter. p. 26

Gib dich zufrieden und sey stille . . . (Be content and remain quiet), unidentified. p. 86

Hier komme ich, mein Hirt! mich durstet nach dir . . . (Here I come, my shepherd, I thirst for thee), unidentified. p. 82

Jesus Christus, unser Heyland . . . (Jesus Christ, our Savior), by Martin Luther. pp. 110, 126

Komm heiliger Geist, Herre Gott . . . (Come Holy Ghost, Lord God), by Martin Luther. p. 24

Lobe den Herrn, den mächtigen König der Ehren . . . (Praise the

Lord, the mighty King of Glory), by Joachim Neander. p. 60; June, note 2

Ringe recht, wenn Gottes Gnade dich nun ziehet und bekehrt . . . (Struggle rightly when God's grace pulls and converts you), by Johann Joseph Winkler. p. 132; July, notes 2, 3

Schwing dich auf zu deinem Gott . . . (Rise up to your God), by Paul Gerhardt. F-T. p. 86

Singt dem Herrn nah und fern, . . . (Sing unto the Lord, both near and far), by Johann Daniel Herrnschmidt. p. 109

So führst du denn recht selig, Herr, die Deinen . . . (Thus thou leadest thy people to salvation, Lord), by Gottfried Arnold. p. 117

Thue als ein Kind und lege dich in deines Vaters Arme . . . (Be as a child and lay thee in thy Father's arms), popular hymn sung in many versions, some of them by Paul Gerhardt. p. 103; Sept. note 7

Treuer Vater, deine Liebe . . . (Loyal Father, Thy love), unidentified. p. 6

Was gibst du dann, o meine Seele? . . . (What do you give then, oh my soul?), by Carl Friedrich Lochner. F-T. 64, p. 114

Welch' ein Sorg und Furcht soll nicht . . . (What a care and fear should not), by Johann Reinhold Hedinger. p. 89

Wir haben eine feste Stadt . . . (We have a fortified city), by Martin Rinkert. F-T. p. 25

Zion, du heilige Gottes-Stadt . . . (Zion, you holy city of God), by Johann Eusebius Schmidt. p. 26

Appendix II

The German-speaking Transports to Georgia 1734–1752

During the past decade several people have asked me to provide them with a list of the various transports, or travel-groups, of German-speaking people. So far I have hesitated to do so, because the available documents are incomplete and woefully inaccurate. However, enough new material has come to light by now to supply cross-references confirming or disproving most questionable records. The following lists have been based, whenever possible, on original ship manifests and have been corroborated by other, preferably German, sources. These transports are designated as Salzburger, Swiss, or Palatine, but it is to be remembered that all these groups included some people not belonging to the dominant group.

The First Salzburger Transport

The first, and most celebrated, of these transports was the first Salzburger transport, which crossed the Atlantic on the *Purrysburg,* Captain Tobias Frye, arriving at Savannah on 12 March 1734. These emigrants had been exiled by the Archbishop of Salzburg for refusing to renounce their Lutheran faith. While the bulk of the exiles had found refuge in Prussia and other Protestant states, some had found shelter in various towns in Swabia, a region northwest of Salzburg. It was from these, and from stragglers who were still crossing the Salzburg border, that the agents of the Lord Trustees recruited the Salzburgers for Georgia. The Salzburger transports were organized by Samuel Urlsperger, the Senior of the Lutheran Ministry in Augsburg.

The first transport, which was organized as a congregation in Augsburg in August of 1733, proceeded on foot to Marksteft on the River Main under the conduct of Baron Philip Georg Friedrich von Reck, a charming but somewhat immature young nobleman. From there they proceeded down the Main and Rhine by boat to Rotterdam, where they met their ministers, Johann

Martin Boltzius, a Prussian, and Christian Israel Gronáu, likewise a North German. With the transport were several other non-Salzburgers, as is indicated below. The present list is based on a poorly recorded manifest, in French, by von Reck, which appears in *Henry Newman's Letterbooks,* ed. George F. Jones, Athens, Ga.: U. of Ga. Press, 1966, pp. 592–593; the inaccuracies were corrected from correct forms in the *Detailed Reports,* especially Vols. VI p. 325 and IX, pp. 6–11. (b. = born, d. = daughter, dd. = died, s. = son, w. = wife)

The names, with birth and death dates when known, are as follows. Unless otherwise noted, all passengers were Salzburgers.

Beque (Becu), Gilbert, a French baker who settled in Savannah.
Boltzius, Johann Martin, Prussian, b. 1703, dd. 1765.
Braunberger, Matthäus, Bavarian, b. 1703, dd. 1734.
Fleiss, Balthasar, b. 1706, dd. 1734.
Gronau, Israel Christian, from Sachsen-Anhalt, b. 1714, dd. 1745.
Gruber, Hans, b. 1688, dd. 1734.
Gruber, Peter, b. 1697, dd. 1740.
Gschwandl, Thomas, b. 1695, dd. 1761.
   Margaretha, w., b. 1710, dd. 1735.
   Margaretha, d., b. 1732, dd. 1761.
Hertzog, Martin, b. 1698, still alive 1750.
Hierl, Maria, b. 1711
Hofer, Anna, b. 1708, dd. 1735.
Huber, Lorentz, b. 1679, dd. 1734.
   (Maria) Magdalena, w., b. 1681, dd. 1734.
   Magdalena, d., b. 1720, dd. 1734.
   Johann, s. Lorentz, b. 1723, dd. 1735.
   Maria, d., b. 1725, dd. 1735.
   Margaretha Huber, d., b. 1728, present 1752.
Kroehr, Catharina, d. Barbara Rohrmoser, b. 1716, married Gronau 1734, married Lemke 1736, dd. 1776
Kroehr, Gertraut, d Barbara Rohrmoser, b. 1719, married Boltzius 1735, still alive 1765.
Lackner, Tobias, b. 1693, dd. 1734.
Leimberger, Christian, b. 1710, dd. 1763.
Mittersteiner, Matthäus, 1692, dd. 1734.

Mosshamer, Johann, b. 1699, dd. 1735.
 Maria, nee Rohrmoser, w., m Peter Gruber 1736.
Ortmann, Christoph, Palatine schoolmaster, ca. 1683, dd. by
 1755.
 Juliana, w., b. ca. 1693, present 1741.
Piedler, Catharina, 1711, married Stephan Rottenberger, alive
 1750.
Rauner, Leonhard, Swabian, b. 1706, dd. 1740.
Rauschgott, Simon, b. 1709, dd. 1735.
Reiter, Maria, b. 1712, dd. 1734.
Reiter, Simon, 1707, present 1757.
Rohrmoser, Barbara, mother of Kroehr girls, b. 1697, dd. 1735.
Roth, Georg Bartholomäus, Bavarian, b. 1688, dd. 1735.
 Maria Barbara, nee Oswald, w., b. 1701, departed 1736.
Schweiger, Georg, b. 1714, dd. after 1774.
Schweighoffer, Paul, b. 1692, dd. 1736.
 Margaretha, nee Pindlinger, w., b. 1692, present 1752.
 Maria, d., b. 1726, marries Christian Riedelsperger II.
 Thomas, s., b. 1729, dd. 1772.
 Ursula, d., b. 1732.
Schweikert, Christian, von Reck's batman, b. 1701, dd. 1735.
Steiner, Christian, b. 1705, dd. 1735.
Zwiffler, (Johann) Andreas, Hungarian German, dd. 1749.

The Second Salzburger Transport

Upon reaching Georgia, the first transport settled at a place
they named Ebenezer, some forty miles northwest of Savannah.
Deceived by appearances, they reported that the area was delightful, fertile, and on a navigable stream; and the enthusiastic
young Baron von Reck returned to Europe determined to take
out a grant there. Consequently, Urlsperger began recruiting
another transport among the Salzburgers residing in Augsburg,
Memmingen, Lindau, Leutkirch, Leibheim, and other South
German cities; and he continued doing so even after distressing
reports began coming in about the poor health, infertile soil,
and inaccessibility of the area chosen for settlement.
 The second transport departed from Augsburg on 23 September 1734 and followed the same route as the first, except that

they stopped off at London instead of at Dover. They were led by a mature Swiss burgher named Jean Vat, who brought them safely to Georgia on the *Prince of Wales*, Georg Dunbar, Captain. They proceeded directly to Ebenezer, which they found in a deplorable condition. In the party were:

Bach, Gabriel, Swabian, killed by Indians 1740.
Bacher, Thomas, bro Balthasar, dd. 1748.
  Maria, nee Schweiger, w.
  Maria, d., b. 1727, married Balthasar Rieser 1752.
  Apollonia, d., b. 1729, present in 1741.
Bishop, Henry, English lad, called Heinrich Bischoff, married (Sibilla) Friederica Unselt of Purysburg, present in 1752.
Brandner, Matthias, present 1759.
  Maria, nee Herl, w., b. 1703, dd. 1768.
  Maria, d., b. 1735, confirmed 1752, married Joseph Schubdrein.
Bruckner, Georg, dd. 1752.
Burgsteiner, Matthias, b. 1695, dd. 1752.
  Agatha, w., dd. 1758
  Johannes, s., present 1741.
  Ruprecht, s., b. 1735, dd. 1740.
Eischperger, Ruprecht, dd. 1762.
  Maria, nee Riedelsperger, w., dd. 68.
Felser, Georg, b. 1686, dd. 1736.
Glantz, Sebastian, b. 1694, dd. 1735.
Hessler (Hössler), Christian, dd. 1766.
Kalcher, Ruprecht, b. ca. 1710, dd. 1752.
Kalcher, Margaretha, nèe Gunther, w. Ruprecht, present 1741.
Kögler, Georg, b. 1708, dd. 1766.
Landfelder, Veit, b. 1717, dd. 1768.
Lemmenhofer, Veit, dd. by 1749.
Madreiter, Hans, b. 1703, dd. 1735.
Maurer, (Hans) Gabriel, b. 1708, dd. 66
Muggitzer, Hans Michael, departed ca. 1735
Ott, (Carl) Sigismund, present 1774
Pichler (Bichler), Thomas, dd. 51
  Margaretha, w., dd. 1738
Resch, Andreas, marries Sibilla Schwab, lost in woods 1735

Riedelsperger, Adam, b. 1698, dd. 1736
  Barbara, w., married Georg Kogler 1737
Riedelsperger, Christian I, s. Adam, dd. 1750
  Christian II, dd. 1760
Riedelsperger, Nikolaus, b. 1688, dd. 1736
Riedelsperger, Ruprecht, still alive 1739
  Anna, w.
Riedelsperger, Stephan
Rieser, Bartholomäus, b. 1682, still alive 1775
  (Anna) Maria, nèe Zugeisen, w., b. 1712, dd. 1737
  Michael, s., b. 1721, departed 1748
  Balthasar, s., b. 1724, wrote will 1775
  Georg, s., d. 1726, dd. 1760
Rottenberger, Stephan, b. 1711, present 1739
  Catharina, nee Piedler, w., alive 1750
Sanftleben, Georg, Silesian, dd. 1749
Schartner, Jacob, still alive 1741
Schoppacher, Ruprecht, b. 1686, dd. 1735
  Maria, w., married Veit Landfelder 1735
  Agatha, d., still alive 1741
Schwab, Sybille, married Andreas Resch 1734
Steiner, Ruprecht, b. 1707, dd. 1752
  Maria, nèe Winter, w., dd. 49
Steiner, Simon, 1698, d. 1740
  Gertraut, nee Schoppacher, w., married Peter Reiter
Zant, Bartholomäus, Swiss, dd. 1745
Zimmerebner, Ruprecht, still alive 1772
Zittrauer, Paulus, dd. 1758

The First Moravian Transport

Ever since the martyrdom of Jan Hus in 1415, dissident Christians had existed underground in Bohemia despite constant persecution. One of these groups, the *Unitas Fratrum,* or Unity of Brothers, was being severely persecuted at the very time that the Archbishop of Salzburg was expelling all Protestants. Since the Habsburgs then owned Bohemia, the Protestants there were oppressed like the Upper Austrians and Carinthians who emigrated to Georgia in 1736. To win religious freedom, some of the

Unitas Fratrum slipped across the border into Saxony, where Count Nikolaus Ludwig von Zinzendorf gave them refuge at an estate named Herrnhut, or "Protection of the Lord." As a result, this small denomination assumed the name Herrnhuters, whereas in America they were known as Moravians, the first refugees having come from the province of Moravia (Mähren) adjoining Bohemia.

Wishing more Germans for their colony, the Trustees resolved on 1 January 35 to give five hundred acres of land to Count Zinzendorf and twenty acres to each of his ten servants upon the expiration of their service. Gottlieb Spangenberg, a leader of the Moravians, sailed on 6 April 1735 with nine co-religionists on the *Two Brothers*, Capt. William Thomson. These were:

Demuth, Gotthard	Rose, Peter
Haberland, Georg	Seifert, Anton
Haberecht, Gottfried	Spangenberg, August Gottlieb
Haberland, Michael	Töltschig, Johann
Riedel, Friedrich	Waschke, Georg

These were joined on 11 October by Jean Regnier, a Swiss of Huguenot parentage.

The Second Moravian Transport

Nearly a year later, on 17 February 1736, the second Moravian transport arrived on the *Simonds,* Capt. Joseph Cornish. These were:

Böhner, Johann	Neisser, Augustin
Böhnisch, Matthias	Neisser, Georg
Demuth, Gottlieb	Nitschmann, David
Regina, w.	Riedel, Catharina, w. Friedrich
Dober, Andreas	Roscher, Heinrich
Maria Catharina, w.	Seybold, Matthias
Frank, Jacob	Tannenberger, David
Haberecht, Rosina w.	Johann, s.
Gottfried	Töltschig, Judith, w. Johann
Jäscke, Juliana	Wascke, Anna, mother
Jag, David	Georg
Mack, Johann Martin	Zeisberger, David
Meyer, Johann Michael	Rosina, w.

Sailing with this party was Capt. Adolf von Hermsdorf, who, as a career officer, could not have been a Moravian. A year later the Moravians were joined by Peter Rose's daughters Anna Catharina and Maria Magdalena; and the following year they were joined by Zeisberger's son David and the latter's companion, Johann Michel Schober and also by Peter Böhler, and Georg Schulius. Refusing to bear arms in the War of Jenkins' Ear, the Moravians left Georgia by 1740.

The First Palatine Transport

Impressed by the good reports about the laborious and docile Salzburgers, the Trustees resolved to send indentured German workers to Georgia, having been disappointed by the urban English emigrants, who were quite unfitted for the hard task of clearing forests. Ever since the great Palatine emigration of 1709–1710, when a disastrous winter and French incursions forced thousands of Palatine peasants to flee their homes, London had been filled with these unhappy people, many of them reduced to begging on the streets after being exploited by recruiters and shippers in Germany and Holland.

On 10 May 1735 the Trustees indentured a number of Palatines to go to Georgia. That is, in return for their passage the Palatines contracted to work a certain number of years for the Trustees, the number of years being given below in parentheses. By this time the word "Palatine" had become a generic word for German workers, even if they were known to be from provinces other than the Rhenish Palatinate. Most of the people on the following list were brought to Georgia on the *James,* Capt. John Yoakley, who made his landfall at Savannah on 1 August 1735. Others traveled on the *Two Brothers* along with the first Moravians, who called them Swiss, and reached Georgia on 6 April, while the remainder traveled on the *Georgia Pink,* Capt. Daubaz, arriving on 27 November.

Bentli (Bandley), Agatha (5)
Christer, Hans Friedrich (5)
    Maria Magdalena , w. (5)
Meyer, Thomas, Swiss, (5), served at Frederica, d. 1740
    Ursula, Swiss, w. (5), moved from Frederica to Ebenezer
    Heinrich, s. (10)

Magdalena, d., moved from Frederica to Ebenezer, married Swiss at mill 1749

Michel, Andreas (5)

Margaretha, w. (5)

Pfitzel ? (Phizzel), Margaretha Maddis, wid Peter (5). The Earl of Egmont gives the mother's name as Maria and adds the names Christian and Dorothy, which do not appear on the 10 May list.

Christian, s.

Barbara, d. (6)

Catharina, d. (11)

Dorothea, d.

Margaretha, d. (2)

Schumacher, Caspar, Swiss from Grisons (5)

Christina, w. (5)

The Third Salzburger Transport

After returning from Georgia, the "Most Delightful Country in the Universe," Baron von Reck traversed Germany in search for colonists for Georgia, no doubt hoping to find workers for the five hundred acres of land he had been granted. He almost persuaded a congregation of Czech exiles to go, but he could not provide them with a Czech-speaking pastor. In Regensburg he was more fortunate, for many Protestant exiles from Upper Austria and Carinthia were residing there in hope of recovering their children, who had been detained in their Catholic homeland. Thus, the third "Salzburger transport" was actually predominantly Austrian, even if von Reck did succeed in recruiting some more Salzburgers in and around Augsburg, to say nothing of other immigrants he picked up in Germany, London, and even Savannah. His party crossed the Atlantic on the *London Merchant*, John Thomas, Captain, and reached Georgia on 17 February 1736. Finding everything in disarray at Ebenezer, they went only as far as the Red Bluff on the Savannah River, where they were joined by the survivors of the first two transports. The name Ebenezer was transferred to the Red Bluff, and the first site was soon known as Old Ebenezer. The list von Reck kept on this voyage was much more reliable than on the first. The passengers were:

Arnsdorff, Andreas Lorentz, Palatine, b.1677, dd. 1737
  (Catharina) Dorothea, w., married Josef Leitner 1741
  Peter, s., b. 1723, received grant 1757
  Sophia, d., b. 1725, present 1741
  Magdalena, d., married Sanftleben 1740
  (Maria) Margaretha, d., b. 1727, present 1741
  (Catharina) Dorothea, d., b. 1730, present 1741
Bauer, Andreas, Austrian, v. 1715, dd. 1736
Christ, Gottfried, Jewish convert, dd. by 1747
Cornberger, Johann, Salz, dd. 1770
Einecker (Einegger), Barbara, Salz, b. 1704, married Leonhard
  Krause 1736
Einecker (Einegger), Gertraud, Salz, b. 1708, married Johann
  Cornberger 1736
Ernst, Josef, Bavarian, b. 1708, dd. 1741
  (Anna) Maria, Bavarian, w., b. 1705, married J. Scheffler 1742
  Sabina, d., b. 1733
  Susanna (Catharina), Bavarian, b. 1735, present 1760
Flerl (Flörl), Carl, Salz, b. 1705, dd. 1764
Flerl, Johann, Salz, b. 1712, dd. 1770
Grimmiger, Andreas, Austrian, b. 1708, departed for Pa. by
  1752
  Sabina, Austrian, w., dd. 1736
Haberfehner, Frantz, Austrian, b. 1686, dd. 1736
  Maria, w., Austrian, b. 1694, dd. 1736
  Maria, d., Austrian, dd. 1736
  Susanna, d., Austrian, b. 1722, present 1741
  Magdalena, d., Austrian, b. 1724, dd. 1740
Helfenstein, (Johann) Jacob, Swiss, 1679, dd. 1736
  (Anna) Dorothea, w., Swiss
  (Maria) Friederica, d., Swiss, 1721, married Ernst Thilo 1739
  (Johann) Friedrich, s., Swiss, b. 1723
  Maria Christina, d., Swiss, b. 1725
  Jeremias, s., Swiss, b. 1725, present 1753
  (Johann) Jacob, s., Swiss, 1727, present 1766
  Johannes, s., Swiss, 1733, present 1763
Herrnberger, Frantz Sigmund, Hungarian German, b. 1698, de-
  parted for Pa. 1740
Holtzer, Susanna, Austrian, b. 1689, dd. 1737

Catharina, Austrian, d., b. 1724, dd. 1751

Höpflinger, (Anna) Maria, Salz, b. 1715, married Hans Flerl 1736

Krause, Leonhard, Salz, b. 1715, dd. 1762

Lackner, Martin, Salz, 1707, present 1752

Leitner, Josef, Austrian, b. 1712, dd. 1767

Maurer, Barbara, Salz, b. 1712

Müller, Friedrich Wilhelm, Franconian, dd. by 1751
   Anna Christina, w., Franconian, present 1751
   (Johann) Simon, s., Franconian, b. 1719, dd. 1737
   (Johann) Paul, s., Franconian, b. 1721, dd. 1775
   (Johanna) Margaretha, d., Franconian, b. 1724, dd. by 1773
   (Agatha) Elisabetha, d., Franconian, b. 1726, present 1739
   (Anna) Maria Magdalena, d., Franconian, b. 1733

Ossenecker (Ossenegger), Thomas, Salz, b. 1711, dd. 1736

Pletter, Johann, Austrian, b. 1705, present 1755

Reiter (Reuter), Peter, Austrian, b. 1715, dd. by 1755

Rieser, (Johann) Michael, Salz, b. 1704, departed 1748
   Anna Maria, Salz, w., b. 1700, dd. 1737
   Gottlieb, Salz, s., b. 1735

Schmidt, Johann, Austrian, b. 1708, dd. 1767
   Catharina, nèe Zehetner, w., Austrian, b. 1705, still alive 1750
   (Johann) Jacob, s., Austrian, b. 1733, dd. 1736

Spielbiegler, Rosina, Salz, b. 1685, dd. 1740
   Johann, s., Salz, departed for Charleston 1740

The Second Palatine Transport

This, the largest of the German transports, was recruited in the summer of 1737, a time when many Germans were clamoring for passage to the Island of Pennsylvania, or willing to go to Georgia in the West Indies. Since the ship's manifest still exists, the number of passengers is quite reliable, even if some names have been distorted beyond recognition. Unlike the Salzburgers, many of these Palatines do not appear in German documents, and therefore the correct forms of their names cannot be ascertained. The party had been badly treated by the Hopes of Rotterdam, notorious dealers in human cargoes, who had broken all promises and packed them in the *Three Sisters* like sardines.

As a result, when they went ashore at Cowes in southern England, they refused to go back aboard until certain conditions were rectified. The Trustees, to whom they were indentured, sent an agent to Cowes to look into their plight; and, after certain reforms were made or promised, they went back aboard, sullen and mutinous. Their captain, Hewitt (first name not recorded), brought them on 21 December to Tybee Island at the mouth of the Savannah River, where they had to remain ten more days for want of a pilot.

Although lumped together as "Palatines," it appears that a good percentage of these passengers were Wurttembergers. The birthdates on the following list are deduced from the ages given by the passengers, who may sometimes have suppressed a few years in the belief that only young people had a good chance to be indentured. This list is based on one by the Earl of Egmont, the foremost Trustee, which is found in the Phillips Collection, Egmont Papers, Vol. 14203, P. II, pp. 156–164.

The names Hier, Hiero, Hierick, and Yorick are taken to be phonetic renderings of Jörg (George). Hier could also be taken as an abbreviation of Hieronymus (Jerome), but the latter rendition is not entirely satisfying, since this name is usually quite infrequent. It will be noted that the only Hieronymus, Hieronymus Staud, appears on the original list as Hieroni Mustout.

"Indentured Servants who Arrived in Georgia on the *Three Sisters,* Capt. Hewitt, on 21 December 1737"

	born
Belli (?) (Bellie), Johannes	1707
Anna, w.	1714
Barbara, d. (dead)	1737
Berrier (Beryer), Johannes	1698
Maria Magdalena, w.	1709
Jörg (Hier), s.	1725
Johann Devolt (Theobald), s.	1727
Margaretha, d.	
Johann Peter, s.	1733
Anna Christina, d.	1735
Blume, Valentin. Serv. to Henry	
Parker	1710

Deigler, Daniel	1692
Maria, w.	1689
Catharina, d.	1724
Maria, d.	1726
Densler, Conrad	1703
Hanna Dorothea, w.	1702
Anna, d.	1726
Heinrich, s.	1728
Regula, d.	1730
Caspar, s.	1734
Hans Jacob, s.	1736
Diehle ? (Dowle), Hans Adam (dead)	1684
Anna, w.	1687
Anna Margaretha, d.	1711
Maria Catharina, d.	1713
Paulser (Paulzer), s.	1715
Peter, s.	1717
Theobald (Teevoult), s.	1733
Erinxmann, Barinkhurf ?	1707 (to Henry
Rebecca, w.	1715 Henriquez)
Fierier ?, Conrad	1711
Christina, w.	1709
Hans Jörg, s. (Yierick)	1735
Jörg Deval, s. (Yierick Levald)	1737
Fitz, Margaretha	Nurse to Trustees'
son	servants
Fritz, Heinrich	1687 (transferred to
Susanna Catharina, d.	1719 Williamson)
Johann, Jörg, s.	1722
Johann Michael, s.	1724
Annabell, d.	1731
Johann Ut ?, s.	1734
Häfner (Havener), Paul	1707
Pieta Clara, w.	1711
Maria Dorothea, d.	1734
Johann Jörg, (Yorick) s.	1735
Hanauer ? (Hanoun, Hanovren),	
Maria Luvis ?, single woman	

Hart, Michael	1692	
Susanna, w.	1683	
Herbach, Jacob	1707	to Abraham
Maria Eva, w.	1709	de Leon
Jung (Young), Jörg (Hier)	1697	
Maria Barbel, w.	1703	
Jörg Peter, s. (Jerick)	1724	
Magdalena, d.	1728	
Margaretha, d.	1729	
Käsemeyer, Martin	1693	
Catharina, w.	1702	
Clemens, s.	1736	
Kemp, Johann	To be surrendered to	
wife, child	Trustees by Henry Parker	
Kieffer (Keifer), Theobald	1692	at cowpen
Maria Cathaina, w.	1692	(Not to be
Margaretha, d.	1717	confused
Jörg David (Hierick Tavid), s.	1719	with Theo-
Mariabell, d.	1724	bald Kieffer
Jörg Friedrich, s.	1730	of Purysburg
Catharina Lies, d.	1732	and Ebenezer)
Jörg Heinrich	1734	
Klause, Leopold	1702	
Anna Catharina, w.	1704	
Johann Michael Simon, s.	1734	
Kraft (Croft, Crost), Peter	1697	to Dr. Graham
Maria Utcroft (?), w.	1697	
Catharina, d.	1724	
Johannes Seldon (?), s.	1729	
Kühler (Kuler, Keeler), Johann Jörg	1692	(Hierick)
Anna Elisabetha, w.	1699	
Maricket (?), d.	1721	
Maria Barbara, d.	1723	
Anna Elisabetha, d.	1725	
Maria Sophia, d.	1728	
Maria Catharina, d.	1730	
Maria Dorothea, d.	1733	
Jörg (Hier) Jacob, s.	1735	

Kurtz (Curts), Jacob	1713
Marold, Peter	1707 to Patrick Houston
Maria Barbell, w.	1713
Jacob, s.	1731
Susanna, d.	1735
Morgan, Maria, single woman	1715
Meyer (Myers), Heinrich	Not to be confused with Heinrich Meyer of German Village on St. Simons
Nungasser (Nongazer), Philip	1682
Annabell, w.	1694
Johann Jacob, s.	1711
Johann Heinrich, s.	1716
Annalies, d.	1720
Anna Catharina, d.	1723
Johann Philip, s.	1732
Johann Martin, s.	1734
Ordner, Jörg (Jerick) Adam	1708
Maria Christina, w.	1709
Maria Elisabetha, d.	1733 (dead)
Johann Jörg Friedrich, s.	1736
Pellihew ?, Johann	1709 to Henry Parker
Elisabetha Barbara, w.	1701
Hans Adam (wife's son)	1719
Anna Dorothea, d.	1721 (Ages do not
Matthis, s.	1723 concur. Perhaps
Susanna, d.	1732 also children of
Conrad, s.	1733 wife)
Plessi, Jacob	1687 (probably Blessi
Anna, w.	1686 from Blasius)
Maria Elisabetha, d.	1716
Anna Ulrich (Urdrick), d.	1727
Radner (Rhodener), Lorentz	1679 To Capt. James
Barbara, w.	1680 Gascoyne
Nikolaus, s.	1716
Maria Barbara, d.	1721
Woolrea (?), d.	1724

Reiter, Carl (Caul)	1707	
Maria Elisabetha, w.	1708	
Johann Philip, s.	1732	
Margaretha, d.	1733	
Johann Michael, s.	1733	
Rhode (?), Hans Jacob	(dead)1707	
Susanna, w. (married Plessi)	1695	
Runsmursha ?, Elisabetha	Single woman, serv. to Nunez Henriquez	
Salice, Anton, Swiss from Grisons	Trustees' gardener	
Catharina, w.		
Anton, s.	1731	
Schäffer, Johann Christoph	1711	to Wm. Ewen
Schneider (Sneyden), Caspar		to Wm. Ewen
Catharina, w.		
Schwartzwälder, Johann	1693	at mill
Anna Maria, w.	1695	
Margaretha, d.	1726	
Mariaket (?), d.	1732	
Hans Michael, s.	1735	
Staude, Hieronymus (Hieroni Mustout)	1682	(dead)
Susanna Margaretha, w.	1687	(dead)
Johannes, s.	1715	
Maria Margaretha, d.	1718	
Steinhübel, Christian	1692	
Apollonia, w.	1692	
Johann Heinrich, s.	1719	
Anna Marabell, d.	1725	
Anna Dorothea, d.	1730	
Anna Elisabetha, d.	1734	
Theiss (Dice), Jacob	1709	at mill
Maria Margaretha, w.	1711	
Tressler, Hans Jörg	1704	to Abraham
Catharina, w.	1710	de Leon
Vipren (?), Maria Barbara	Single woman, to Mr. Williamson	

Wannemacher (Vanomaker), Johann

Jacob   1716 to Mr. Williamson
                                                  (or to Hanss Jacob
                                                  Ham)

The Third Palatine Transport

The Palatines who arrived in Georgia on 1 October 1738 dif-
fered from previous emigrants in being redemptioners rather
than indentured servants. That means that, instead of being
contracted to their future employers before leaving Europe,
they sold their service for a number of years directly to the ship's
captain, who re-sold it in America to settlers in need of labor.
This type of contract, first begun by Zachary Hope in 1728, was
more efficient and became very popular. Capt. William Thomson carried many Germans to Georgia "at his own risque," as the
Trustees expressed it.

		born	
Adde, Salomo, Swabian shoemaker.		1705.	Ebenezer
Margaretha, w.		1706	
Johann, s.		1735	
Bender, Christoph, Pal.		1692	to James
Elisabetha, niece		1714	Habersham
Bineker, Johann Friedrich, Pal.		1703	to Andreas Walser
Christina, d.		1728	at Frederica
Johann Ulrich, s.		1731	
Bischoff, Anna Maria, Pal. wid,		1699	Ebenezer
Clemens, Widow, Pal.		1703	Frederica
Cluer, Elisabetha, Pal.		1705	
Custabader, Catharina, Pal.		1688	Ebenezer
Derick, Widow, Pal.		1712	
Elisabetha, d.		1730	
Melchior, s.		1731	
Jacob, s.		1733	
Margaretha, d.		1737	
Gebhart, Magdalena, Pal.		1712	Ebenezer
Elisabetha, sister.		1724	
Eva, sister		1728	
Gebhart, Philip, Pal.		1693	Frederica
Martha, w.		1695	

Maria Catharina, d.	1721	
Philip, s.	1732	
Hans Georg, s.	1736	
Guring, Simon, Pal.	1706	to Fallowfield
Anna Maria, w.	1708	
Heldt, Conrad, Pal.	1686	public
Elisabetha, w.	1685	garden,
Hans Michael, s.	1715	later to
Elisabetha, d.	1721	Ebenezer
Heinrich, Peter, Swab.	1690	Ebenezer
Juliana, w.	1684	
Eva (Barbara), d.	1716	
(Anna) Catharina, d.	1718	
(Anna) Magdalena, d.	1719	
(Hanna) Margaretha, d.	1723	
Johann Georg, s.	1727	
Holland, Johann Georg, Pal.	1716	
Huber, Blasius, Pal.	1710	
Ichinger, Jacob, Pal.	1689	Frederica
Catharina, w.	1685	
Sophia, d.	1720	
Hans Michael, s.	1724	
Annalies, d.	1729	
Jacob, s.	1733	
Kensler ?, Christoph, Pal.	1695	Frederica
Agnes Christina, w.	1699	
Anna Margaretha, d.	1726	
Bastian (Sebastian), s.	1735	
Knowart, Kunegunda, Pal. widow	1684	
Krämer, (Johann) Christoph, Pal.	1689	to James
Clara, w.	1695	Habersham
Anna Maria, d.	1724	
Christoph, s.	1726	
Kremp, Johann, Pal.	1703	
Sophia, w.	1698	
Catharina, d.	1728	
Maria Magdalena, d.	1731	
Johann Ulrich, s.	1734	
Anna Margaretha, d.	1736	

Leonhard, Johann, Pal.	1719	to Rev. Norris
Löwenberger, Christian, Pal.	1706	Ebenezer, then
Margaretha, w.	1703	Savannah
Müller, Johann Adam, Pal.	1690	to James
Christina, w.	1708	Habersham
Veronica, d.	1722	
Philip, s.	1724	
Johann Nikolaus, s.	1726	
Maria Catharina, d.	1728	
Müller, Leonhart, Pal.	1697	to Noble Jones
Eva, w.	1698	
Hans Michael, s.	1725	
Hans Bernhard, s.	1732	
Nett, Friedrich, Pal.	1707	Ebenezer
Elisabetha, w.	1702	
Pickli, Hans Georg, Pal.	1695	Frederica
Agnes, w.	1699	
Johann, s.	1721	
Thomas, s.	1725	
Jacob, s.	1732	
Ragnous, Johann, Pal.	1704	Frederica
Margaretha, w.	1702	
Johann, s.	1726	
Anna Maria, d.	1730	
Ruf (Roof), Jacob, Pal.	1690	Frederica
Jacob, s.	1717	
Margaretha, d.	1731	
Schantz, Christoph, Pal.	1717	to Henry Parker
Wilhelm, brother	1722	
Schantz, Johann Peter, Pal.	1696	Frederica
Anna Maria, w.	1697	
Anna Magdalena, d.	1720	
Hans Adam, s.	1726	
Carl, s.	1731	
Andreas, s.	1734	
Philip, s.	1736	
Schlechtermann, Johann, Pal.	1688	Ft. Argyle
Anna Barbara, w.	1698	
Margaretha Barbara, d.	1719	

Josef Michael, s.	1720	
Johann Peter, s.	1722	
Juliana, d.	1727	
Georg Bartholomäus, s.	1728	
Johann Lorentz, s.	1730	
Georg Moritz, s.	1731	
Margaretha, d.	1738	
Schmidt, Johann, Pal.	1694	to Mr. Mouse
Schneider? (Taylor), Abraham, Pal.	1718	Ebenezer
Schneider, Michael, Pal.	1698	Ebenezer
Anna, w.	1708	
Hans Georg, s.	1726	
Johann, s.	1732	
Schönbacher (Shanebaker), Pal. wid.	1702	Frederica
Hans Michael, s.	1730	
Hans Georg, s.	1731	
Magdalena, d.	1735	
Straube, Adam, Pal.	1701	Vernonburg, then Ebenezer
Upshaw (?), Josef, Pal?	1722	to Mackintosh Moore
Victor, Widow, Pal.	1702	Frederica
Anna, d.	1718	
Peter, s.	1721	
Annalies, d.	1722	
Jacob, s.	1728	
Sule, s.	1731	
Waldhauer (Volthoward), Andreas, Pal.	1689	Frederica
Anna, w.	1697	
Tobias, s.	1726	
Hans Georg, s.	1729	
Waldhauer (Volthoward), Barbara, Pal.	1724	Ebenezer
Waldhauer (Volthoward), Margaretha	1717	Ebenezer
Wagonerak (?), Johann Clemens, Pal.	1690	
Catharina, w.	1715	
Wüller, Hans Michael, Pal.	1702	to Fallowfield
Maria, w.	1702	

The Sanftleben Party

In 1739 a small contingent joined the Salzburgers at Ebenezer, these being tradesmen and marriageable women recruited by Georg Sanftleben, a Silesian carpenter who had returned home to fetch his sister Elisabetha. This small party occasioned voluminous correspondence to and from the Trustees. In the group were:

Berenberger, Margaretha, married Ruprecht Zimmerebner 1740
Egger, Margaretha, married Ulich and then Martin Lackner, both in 1739
Lackner, Elisabetha, sister of Martin, dd. 1739
Sanftleben, (Anna) Elisabetha, b. 1698, married Michael Schneider 1740
Sanftleben, Georg
Ulich, Johann Caspar, d. 1739
Wassermann, Elisabetha, married Johann Pletter 1739

The Fourth Salzburger Transport

Realizing that their settlement needed more inhabitants, and being greatly in need of hired hands, the Salzburgers of Ebenezer sent a petition to the Lord Trustees in 1939 to send them another transport. This the Trustees agreed to do; but this time, instead of supplying provisions, the Trustees promised a monetary support for the first sixth months. This stipulation was most agreeable to the inhabitants of Ebenezer, who by now had sufficient food for the newcomers but very little cash with which to buy necessities. The new emigrants, recruited from the Salzburger exiles residing in Swabian cities, left from the port of Canstadt on the Neckar, proceeded to Rotterdam, and then on to Georgia, where they arrived on 2 December 1741. The voyage was healthy, but many of these unseasoned immigrants died of fever the following summer. This list is based on the original specification as it appears in the unpublished Vol. XXX (pp. 374–376) of the *Colonial Records of the State of Georgia,* which is housed in the Georgia Historical Society in Savannah. The many mistakes of the English scribe have been corrected from Boltzius' list of recipients of gifts in the *Detailed Reports*, Vol. IX, pp. 13–15. All but Vigera and the Scheraus family were Salzburgers.

	born
Bacher, Balthasar, carpenter	1710
Anna Maria, w.	1709
Bacher, Matthäus, farmer	1686
Christina, w.	1693
Brückl (Brickelin), single	1719
Crell, Walburga, single. Step-	
daughter of Bernhard Glocker	1723
Eigel, Georg, farmer	1701
Ursula, w.	1700
Anna Theresa, d.	1718
Lorentz Ludwig, s.	1730
Anna Maria, d.	1733
Johann Lorentz, s.	1735
Johann Frantz, s.	1737
Samuel, s. (died en route)	1740
Eischberger, David, miller	1717
Anna Maria, w.	1711
Glaner (Klamer), Georg, farmer	1704
Gertraut, w.	1703
Glocker, Bernhard, farmer	1703
Elisabetha, w.	1698
Gertraut, d.	1732
Eva, d.	1734
Sebastian, s.	1737
Paul, s.	1741
Graniwetter, Caspar, brewer	1705
Anna Catharina, w.	1718
Haberer, Michael, brick-	
layer & farmer	1714
Anna Barbara, w.	1701
Johann Christoph, s., born	
en route	1741
Häussler, Christina, single	1721

Kocher, Johann Georg,
    weaver & husbandman   1701
    Maria Helena, w. (Boltzius calls
    her Apollonia)   1697
    Georg, s.   1732
Kohleisen, Peter, shoemaker   1701
    Maria, w.   1692
Kreder (Koeder), Apollonia, single 1709
Künlin, Conrad (called Kunej by
    Vigera), died upon arrival   1699
    Maria, w.   1707
    Johannes, s.   1739
Lackner (Lechner), Martin, farmer 1712
    Catharina Barbara, w.   1719
Lechner, Veit, locksmith   1713
    Magdalena, w.   1693
    Elisabetha, d.   1731
Maurer, Johannes, carpenter   1715
    Maria, w.   1715
Meyer (Mayer), Johann Georg,
    glover   1720
Meyer (Mayer) Johann Ludwig,
    surgeon, brother   1715
    Elisabetha, nee Müller, w.   1715
Meyer (Mayer), Maria, widow,
    d. of Matthäus Bacher   1718
Piltz, Andreas, carpenter   1705
    Sybilla, w.   1714
Rieser, Simon, farmer   1685
    Magdalena, w.   1705
Roner, Magdalena, single,
    married Georg Meyer 1742   1712
Scheffler, Johannes,
    weaver & husbandman   1714
    Catharina, w.   1715
    Johannes, s.   1735
Scheraus, Johann, Swab.   1706
    Maria Helena, nee Gott, w.   1697
    Johann, s.   1735

Schrempf, Ruprecht, locksmith.
    Stepson of Veit Lechner   1722
Steinbacher, Barbara, single   1719
Vigera, Johann Friedrich, Alsatian   1706

The First Swiss Transport

Whereas the fourth Salzburger transport crossed the Atlantic safely and with no deaths, the first Swiss transport fared less well, in fact about a third the passengers on the *Europa,* Capt. John Wadham, died of "Palatine Fever," and there were hardly enough able-bodied passengers and crewmen to throw the corpses overboard. Even after the *Europa* reached Tybee Island on 4 December 1741, the wretched survivors had to remain some days on the ship in quarantine. As a result, nearly a third more died on shipboard or in Georgia. Most of the passengers had been destined for South Carolina, but the survivors were treated so well by the Trustees that many of them could be persuaded to remain in Georgia. The list is found in the *Colonial Records of the State of Georgia,* Vol. 30, pp. 393–399.

	born	
am Stein (Arnstein), Caspar, tailor	1713	
(Anna) Maria, w.	1713	
Beltz, Hans Ulrich, weaver	1711	Vernonburg
Margaretha, w.	1718	
Elisabetha, d.	1739	
Boltschauser ?, Jacob, carpenter	1696	
Ursula, w.	1696	
Elias, s.	1735	
Hans Jacob, s.	1736	
Heinrich, s.	1737	
Burckhart, Adrian, farmer	1698	
Catharina, w.	1703	
Adrian, s.	1729	
Hans Jacob, s.	1730	
Susanna, d.	1734	
Burckhart, Hans Georg, farmer	1723	
Anna Maria, sister	1724	
Johannes, brother	1730	

Burgemeister, Christoph, silk worker	1709	Vernonburg
Elisabetha, w.	1707	
Martin, s.	1741	d. 1741
Christoph, s.	1737	
Hans Ulrich, s.	1740	
Burgi, Rudolf, woodman	1691	Vernonburg
Esther, w.	1691	d. 1741
Rudolf, s.	1722	
Anna, d.	1728	
Anna Margaretha, d.	1730	d. 1741
Hans Kunrath, s.	1731	d. 1741
Esther, d.	1735	
Calliser (Collifer), Anna Maria, single	1719	
Calliser, Hans Caspar, ropemaker	1717	
Danner, Jacob, tinker	1706	Vernonburg
Barbara, w.	1716	
Engeli, Hans Jacob, farmer	1709	
Anna, w.	1707	
Jacob, s.	1734	
Gebhart, Hans Heinrich, cooper	1696	
Catharina, w.	1711	
Samuel, s.	1719	
Susanna, d.	1721	
Magdalena, d.	1731	
Anna, d.	1735	d. 1741
Anna Maria, d.	1740	d. 1741
Hag, Johannes Ulrich, smith	1695	
Anna Maria, w.	1695	
Johannes, s.	1721	
Barbara, d.	1723	
Maria, d.	1725	
Hans Jacob, s.	1728	
Hans Ulrich, s.	1730	
Hans Michael, s.	1732	
Verena, d.	1735	
Hag, Hans Ulrich, carpenter	1708	

Maria, w.	1708	
Catharina, d.	1732	
Hans Jacob, s.	1736	
Halter, Hans Kunrath, bricklayer	1797	
Barbara, w.	1710	
Barbara, d.	1737	
Anna, d.	1739	
Halter, Hans Kunrath, locksmith	1703	
Elisabetha, w.	1699	
Martha, d.	1730	
Ulrich, s.	1731	
David, s.	1733	
Barbara, d.	1735	
Catharina, d.	1738	
Häner, Nikolaus, shoemaker	1705	Vernonburg
Elisabetha, w.	1703	
Nikolaus, s.	1726	
Johannes, s.	1730	
Margaretha, d.	1732	
Elisabetha, d.	1734	
Josef, s.	1737	d. 1741
Verena, d.	1740	d. 1741
Juker, Hans Adam, farmer	1696	
Barbara, w.	1708	d. 1741
Kress, Hans Kurath, laborer	1696	d. 1741
Elisabetha, w.	1699	d. 1741
Verena, d.	1719	
Elisabetha, d.	1721	d. 1741
Heinrich, s.	1729	d. 1741
Friedrich, s.	1734	d. 1741
Kuntz, Hans Jacob, schoolmaster	1701	d. 1741
Maria, w.	1701	d. 1741
Margaretha, d.	1729	d. 1741
Hans Jacob, s.	1730	d. 1741
Erhart, s.	1733	d. 1741
Hans Heinrich, s.	1738	d. 1741
Kuradi, Hans Kunrath, farmer	1699	d. 1741
Anna Barbara, w.	1701	Vernonburg

Heinrich, s.	1721	
Adam, s.	1727	
Hans Kurath, s.	1738	
Lang, Abraham, smith	1695	
Barbara, w.	1704	
Anna Maria, d.	1730	
Hans Kunrath, s.	1734	
Lauchenauer (Egmont has Landenauer), millwright	1717	
Lichliege (Lichliebe), Hans Heinrich, farmer	1707	
Anna, w.	1707	
Anna, d.	1730	
Barbara, d.	1739	
Riemensperger, Hans Jacob (conductor of party)	1699	
Riegler, Leonhard, butcher	1716	
Catharina, w.	1722	
Schad, Hans Joachim, smith	1691	Vernonburg
Eva, w.	1694	
Anna, d.	1717	
Salomo, s.	1723	
Hans Joachim, s.	1725	
Margaretha, d.	1729	
Schneider (Schreyder), Adam, drummer	1719	
Schneider (Snyder), Heinrich, laborer	1711	
Elisabetha, w.	1711	d. 1741
Anna Barbara, his sister	1712	
Sigerist, Hans Martin, farmer	1706	
Anna, w.	1703	
Johannes, s.	1729	
Hans Martin, s.	1734	
Hans Jacob, s.	1736	d. 1741
Hans Kunrath, s.	1737	d. 1741
Stelli, Hans Georg (Schad's son-in-law)	1719	
Stoll, Ezechiel, smith	1711	Vernonburg

(Anna) Magdalena, w.	1713	
Jacob, s.	1741	
Strubler, Hans Jacob, ropemaker	1719	
Elisabetha, w.	1715	d. 1741
Stutz, Hans, farmer	1701	Vernonburg
Barbara, w.	1701	
Michael, s.	1732	
Hans Caspar, s.	1734	d. 1741
Hans Heinrich, s.	1735	d. 1741
Hans Jacob, s.	1738	d. 1741
Hans Ulrich, s.	1740	d. 1741
Torgler (Turkler, etc.),		
Johannes, farmer	1714	Vernonburg
Catharina, w.	1708	
Anna, d.	1740	
Vetterli, Heinrich, farmer	1701	d. 1741
Catharina, w.	1701	d. 1741
Hans Jacob, s.	1730	d. 1741
Anna Magdalena, d.	1731	
Regula, d.	1735	
Vogler, Hans Ulrich, glazier	1703	
Anna Maria, w.	1702	
Anna Magdalena	1730	
Heinrich, s.	1732	
Hans Caspar, s.	1738	
Hans Ulrich, s.	1739	
Wachter, Josephus, shoemaker	1705	Vernonburg
Susanna, w.	1709	
Elisabetha, d.	1735	
Susanna, d.	1738	
Willer, Maria Eurich (Eirtsch),		
cousin of Würli	1720	
Wögli (Wrogeley), Hans Jacob,		
cooper	1701	
Rachel, w.	1701	
Anna Barbara, d.	1723	
Johannes, s.	1730	
Anna Maria, d.	1731	
Würli (Wierley, Wurly), Hans		

Caspar, weaver	1696
Margaretha, w.	1701
Elisabetha, d.	1721
Hans Jacob, s.	1726
Margaretha, d.	1735
Wirth (Würth), Hans Jacob, tailor	1693
Catharina, w.	1708
Salamena, d.	1729
Anna, d.	1730
Catharina, d.	1732
Elisabetha, d.	1735
Susanna, d.	1739

The Fourth Palatine Transport

The fourth Palatine transport was recruited from a party of Germans who had departed for Pennsylvania a year earlier at their own expense. Unfortunately for them, war was being waged between England and Spain, and two Spanish corsairs intercepted them just off the coast of England and took them to Bilbao. When the British finally ransomed them, those who were able to do so chose to return to Germany, but a hundred or more who could not afford to do so agreed to go to Georgia and to earn their passage by working for the Trustees. As in the case of the *Europa*, fever also broke out on their ship, the *Judith*, and took the captain and mate, many sailors, and several prominent Englishmen. Strangely, it did not take many of the German passengers; and the Swiss pastor Bartholomäus Zouberbühler was able to guide the ship safely to Frederica, where it landed on 22 January 1746. Most of the passengers continued on to Savannah, where some were employed by the Trustees and by certain individuals, while the remainder were assigned to Boltzius and Michael Burckhalter, the most prominent Swiss settler. A very anglicized ship list is found in the *Colonial Records of the State of Georgia*, Vol. 31 (unpublished), pp. 45–48. On the *Judith* were:

Bormann (Boorman), Johann Michael
  Maria Eva, w.
Brachfeld ? (Brakefield), Johann Wendel
  Elisabetha, w.

Hermann (Harman), Jacob
  Dorothea, w.
Ihle ? (Illy), Jacob
  Agnes, w.
  Andreas, s.   1732
  Wilhelm, s.   1735
  Michael, s.
  Jacob, s.
Jäckli ? (Yakeley), Jacob, apprentice
                to Bormann   1739
Knippling, Anna Catharina
  Martin, s.   1732
  Anna Margaretha, d.   1736
  Jacob, s.   1739
  Anna Catharina, d. 1743   1743
Kusmaul (Kusmoul), Jacob
  Sevila, w.
Leinebacher (Linebaker), Georg
  Adam   1735
  Salma, sister (Ebenezer)   1734
Litola, Nicolas, Grisons?, Piedmont?
Mück (Mick), Jonas
  Anna Maria, w.
Müller (Miller), Malachi
  Margaretha, w.
Pett, Hans Georg
  Catharina, w.
  Rosina, d. b. 1737
  Michael, s. b. 1733
  Caspar, s
Ports, Jacob (Ebenezer)
  Magdalena, w. (Ebenezer)
Ports, Johann Philip
Raag ? (Raagin), Barbara
Ratien, Maria (sister-in-law of Wüst)
  Anna Dorothea, d.   1738
Ritschart ? (Richard), Thomas
  Elisabetha, w.
  Michael, s.   1729

Peter, s.	1732
Lorentz, s.	1736
Iscariot, s. (ran away from Ebenezer)	
Wilhelm, s. (ran away from Ebenezer)	

Schaaf, Ulrich
Steheli ? (Staley), Johann
   Maria, w.

Gottlieb, s.	1729
Philip Jacob, s.	1733
Friedrich, s.	1735

   Johann, s.
   Magdalena, d.
Treutlen (Frideling), Maria Clara

Johann Adam, s. (Ebenezer)	1733

   Friedrich, s.
Ulmann, Conrad Philip, apprentice

to Brachfeld	1738

Voltz (Follz), Johann Martin
Walthauer (Walthour), Johann Caspar

Johann Caspar, s.	1731
Georg Michael, s.	1732

Walthauer (Walthour), Christoph Conrad
Walthauer (Walthour), Georg Jacob
Walthauer (Walthour), Margaretha Barbara
Weissenbacher (Wyssenbakher), Jacob
   Margaretha, w.
Weissengert ? (Wyssengert), Anna Maria
Wüst (West), Matthias
   Magdalena, d.
   Catharina, mother of Matthias
Zorn (Zoning), Margaretha
   Barbara, sister

The Fifth Palatine Transport

Because the Salzburgers had lost most of their children and
were therefore in desperate need of hired hands to help them in
their farming, the Trustees agreed to send them some inden-

tured servants, and also some free men who would pay their own passage. The party arrived on the *Charles Town Galley*, Peter Bogg captain, on 2 October 1749. Some were indentured to individual settlers and some to the mill, one married his master's daughter, and three ran away to Congarees in South Carolina. The following list is based on a report by Boltzius, which appears in the *Colonial Records of the State of Georgia*, Vol. 26 (unpublished), pp. 49–51.

Baumann, Conrad, serv. to Matthias Brandner, dd.   1749
Blessing, Leonhard, serv. to Johann Maurer
Bunz, Johann Georg, serv. to Christian Leimberger
Burckhart, Martin, serv. to Christian Leimberger
Dechtli, Johann Georg, married his master's daughter and settled here.
Dellinger, Christoph, serv. to Ruprecht Zimmerebner
Heidt, Georg, serv. to Simon Reiter
Kaup, Jacob, serv. to mill
     Barbara, w.
Kohler, Barbara, serv. to Leonhard Krause
Kugel, Johann, bought his freedom and settled in Ebenezer.
Kugel, Matthias," " " " " " " " " " "
Kühn, Balthasar, ran away and settled at Congarees.
Lamprecht, Johann Georg, serv. to Ruprecht Steiner
     Anna Maria, w.
     Andreas, s.
Michler, Jost, serv. to Josef Leitner
Mohr, Jacob, serv. to Christian   1700
     Riedelsperger
     Anna Maria, w.
     Christina, d., married Andreas Seckinger
     small child
     small child
Rentz, Johann Georg, serv. to Matthias Burgsteiner
Scheffer, Johann Friedrich, ran away to Congarees
Schneider, (Anna) Barbara (sister to Catharina), serv. to Paul Zittrauer
Schneider, (Maria) Catharina (sister to Barbara), serv. to Martin Lackner

Schubdrein, Daniel, from Weiher in Saarbrücken, bought free-
  dom from Zouberbuhler and settled in Ebenezer
Schubdrein, Josef, " " " " " " " " " "
Schubdrein, (Johann) Peter, 1714 " " " " " " " "
Seckinger, Andreas (bro Matthias), serv. to Boltzius
  Catharina, nee Seckinger, w.
  five small children
Seckinger, Lucia (sister of Andreas
  & Matthias), serv. to Boltzius   1727
Seckinger, Matthias, serv. to Boltzius
  Anna Catharina, w.
  Johann Georg, s.   1744
  Anna, d.   1747
  Samuel, s.
  Jonathan, s.
  Hanna Elisabeth
Seelmann, Johann Christian, physician, moved to Pennsylvania
Weber, (Georg) Michael, serv. to Johann Flerl
Wirtsch (later Wertsch), Johann Caspar, serv. to Thomas
  Gschwandl and schoolmaster on plantations
Ziegler, Johann Georg, serv. to Thomas Gschwandl
Zoller, Johann Balthasar, serv. to mill, ran away to Congarees
  Rosina, w.

The First Swabian Transport

The Salzburgers' constant request for servants encouraged
the Trustees to send them another transport, and Urlsperger
began recruiting throughout Wurttemberg, especially in the
area of Leibheim in the Territory of Ulm. On 29 October 1750
Capt. Charles Leslie of the *Charming Martha* arrived in Georgia
with the following passengers.

Bader, Matthias, returns to Germany
Bollinger, Georg, serv. to Ruprecht Steiner, gr. 48
Botzenhardt, Barthel, from Langenau, returns to Germany
Botzenhardt, Martin, from Langenau, returns to Germany
Fetzer, ... , Widow of Abraham Fetzer, who died in passage.
  She bought her freedom and worked on mulberry trees.

Christian, s., serv. to Ruprecht Schrempf   1740
daughter, with mother   1743
Fetzer, Sebastian
  Ursula, w.   1719
  Anna, d.
Fetzer, Ulrich
  Barbara, w.   1720
Heinle, Johann, from Gaersteten, serv. at sawmill, dd. 1751
  wife (Barbara, b. 1709, dd. 1756 ?)
  Johann, s., serv. to Georg Glaner
  Jacob, s., serv. to Johann Schmidt
Helmle, Nikolaus, from Albeck, serv. to Martin Lackner, Sr.
  Maria Magdalena, w.
Herzog, Georg (died in passage)
Huber, Anna, a girl of ten years, serv. to Georg Meyer 1740
Huber, Helena, serv. to Leonhard Krause
Huber, Jacob, from Langenau, settles on own land
  wife
  small daughter
  small daughter
  small daughter
Huber, Sara, serv. to Johann Cornberger
Jünginger, Abraham, single, serv. in Sav.
Meyer, Johann (died in passage)
Michel, Catharina, from Nerenstetten, accompanies Jacob
  Huber
Neidlinger, Johann, sets up tannery
  Johann II, s.
Neidlinger, Ulrich, s. Johann
  Ulrich II, s.
Oechsele, Barbara, from Langenau, accompanies Jacob Huber
Paultisch, (Johann) Philip
  Anna Magdalena, w.
Rahn, Caspar, grant Briar Creek 1752
Rahn, Conrad, from Ulm
  (Anna) Barbara, w. nee Paulitsch
  Jacob, s. b. 1722
Scheraus, (Johann) Georg, from Bermeringen by Ulm, re-
  turned to Germany

Scheraus, Johann I, b. 1686, from Bermeringen
  Maria Helena, nee Gott, b. 1697, w.
Scheraus, Johann II, s. 1706, s. Johann I, from Bermeringen
  Johann III, s. b. 1735
Scheraus, Magdalena (w. Johann II ?), grant 1752
Schleicher, Georg, serv. to Ruprecht Eischberger
Schlumberger, Abraham, from Setzingen, died 1750 in
  Savannah
Slumberger, Jacob, from Setzingen, died in passage
  Maria, nee Gröner, wid., marries widower at Vernonburg
  small child
  small child
Söldner, Martin, widower, buys freedom, marries Barbara
  Oechsle

The Second Swabian Transport

Unfortunately there is no ship manifest for the second or third Swabian transports, the names below are largely based on references in the *Ackerwerck Gottes,* correspondence in the *Colonial Records,* and contemporary land grants. The names bearing asterisks are those of spokesmen presented to the Trustees on 12 August 1751. It is assumed that their families, recorded elsewhere, were on the same ship, although it is possible that one or more came with the next transport, as seems to have been the case of Barbara Oechsele, who may have been sent as a scout on the previous transport. The second Swabian transport was conducted by a talented surveyor named de Brahm, who settled his charges at Bethany, a few miles upstream from Ebenezer.

Brahm, (Johann) Wilhelm (Gerhard) de, from Koblenz,
  conductor
  Wilhelmina de, w.
Gerber, Paul, from Albeck
Gnann, Jacob, from Langenau, bro Georg   1708
Gnann*, (Johann) Georg, from Langenau   1704
  Anna, nee Gress, w.
  Andreas, s.   1745
  Michael, s.   1747
  Jacob, s.   1749

Hackel, Jörg, from Holtzkirch
Haisler, David (54 late from Germany)
Hammer, Peter, from Chemnitz in Saxony
    Anna Rosina, w.   1717
    Elisabetha, d.   1743
Hasenlauer, Sebastian, from Langenau
Kraft, David, merchant from Ravensburg
    Anna Barbara, nee Brant, w., married Rabenhorst 1753
Mack, Wolfgang, from Langenau
Neibling, Alexander, grant Briar Creek 1752
Neibling, Bartholomäus, from Langenau
Oechsele, Christian, s. Melchior
    Angelika, w.
Oechsle*, Johann, from Langenau, s. Michael
Oechsele, (Johann) Melchior, grant 1752, dd. 1753
    (Johann) Michael, s.
    Maria Christina, d.
Oechsele, Michael
    Maria, d. married J. G. Niess 1755
Remshard*, Daniel, from Langenau
    Margaretha, w.
Schröder, Anna, from Langenau
Schubdrein, Daniel, b. 1682
    Margaretha, w. b. 1685
    Johann Peter, s. (returning to Ebenezer after a visit home to
    Nassau-Saarbrücken, now Weiher or Weyer in Lorraine)
Slesing, (Johann) Leonhard
Tussing (Duseign), Jacob
Unselt, David, from Bernstadt
Walliser*, Michael
    Elisabetha, w.
Weinkauf*, Michael
    Maria, w.
Weinkauf, Matthias
    Maria, w.
Winckler, (Hans) Georg, from Niederstotzingen
Ziegler, Agnesia, nee Hermann
    Eva Maria, d, married Johann Caspar Bothe 1754
    Johann Michel, s.

Zipperer, Christian (Jonathan), from Bernstadt
  Anna Maria, w.
  Jonathan, s.
  Peter, s.

The Third Swabian Transport

Pleased with the results of the first two Swabian transports, the Trustees asked Urlsperger to form a third; and this party reached Georgia late in November of 1752 with a Capt. Brown, the name of whose ship has not been recorded. They must have hurried to take out grants, since many of them received grants before the year was out. They were supposed to settle at Halifax, some fifty miles upstream from Ebenezer, and their grants were mostly made out accordingly. However, settlement so far away proved unfeasible, and a majority removed to Bethany or Savannah. The most important man in the party was Capt. (Stückhauptmann) Thomas Krause, who denied that he was in charge yet was obliging enough to help Boltzius look out for them. The year of a first grant is given when there would otherwise be some doubt as to identity.

Daumer, Michel, from Langensee
Eberhard, Johann, grant 1752
Eckhart, Martin, from Nerenstetten, serv. to Dauner
Eckhart, Ursula
Ehrhard, Johann, from Altheim
Fischer, Georg, from Langenau
  Anna Catharina, w., b. 1728
Fischer, Michael, grant 1752
Fischer, Nikolaus, grant 1752
Frey, Abraham, from Bermeringen
Greiner, Johann Caspar I (probably of 3rd transport)
  Caspar II, s. grant 1752
Greiner, (Johann) Martin I, grant 1752
  (Johann) Martin II
Greiner, Maria Magdalena, married Michael Weber 1754
Gröner, Barbara, from Altheim

Gross, Michael, from Leutzhausen, grant 1752
Hagemeyer, Juliana, from Blaubeyern, grant 1752
  Euphrosyna, d., d. 1753
Hasenlauer, Sebastian, from Langenau
Hirschmann, (Johann) Caspar II, grant Halifax 1752
  (Johann) Caspar II, s., grant Halifax 1752
  Barbara, d.
Lange, Georg, grant 1752
Lange, Gottlieb, grant 1752
Lange, Johann I, grant Briar Creek 1752
  Johann II, s., grant 1752
Lohrmann, Johann, from Ulm
Mack, Bartholomäus, b. 1730
  Maria, w.
Mack, Thomas, grant Bethany 1759
Mack, Wolfgang, from Langenau
Mayer, Johann I, from Riedheim, grant 1752
  Johann II, s., married Christina Remshard
  Hanna (Anna) married David Unselt
Mayer, Paul, from Bermeringen, grant 1752
Neibling (Niebling, Nübling), Alexander, grant Briar Creek
  1752
Neibling (Niebling, Nübling), Bartholomäus, from Langenau
Niess, (Johann) Georg, serv. to Boltzius, grant Bethany 1753
Niess, (Johann) Leonhard, grant 1752
Niess, Margaretha, b. 1707
Niess, Martin, grant 1752
Pflüger, Johann I, from Langenau, grant 1752
Piltz, Sigismund, grant 1754
  Anna, w.
Rabenhorst, Christian, from Poggenköp in Hinterpommern,
  b. 1728
Rau, Anna Catharina, b. 1697, mother of Georg, grant 1752
  Barbara, d., m. Hans Pflüger
  (Johann) Georg, from Leipheim, s. Anna Catharina, grant
  1752
Salfner, Matthias I, from Moergelstetten, grant 1752
  Agatha, w. b. 1712

Matthias II, s. b. 1737
(Georg) Leonhard, s. b. 1739, grant 1752
Anna Margaretha, d. b. 1740
Jacob, s. b. 1745
Salfner, (Johann) Adam (s. Matthias I ?), grant 1752
Salfner, Michael (s. Matthias I ?), grant 1759
Schneider, Andreas, from Freudenberg, grant Black Creek 1752

 *NOTES*

INTRODUCTION

1. For greater detail, see George F. Jones, *The Salzburger Saga*, Athens, Ga.: University of Georgia Press, 1983.

JANUARY

1. Only fifteen were reported in *Ausführliche Nachrichten* for 1742.

2. Boys generally had to serve to the age of twenty-one, girls to the age of eighteen.

3. Here *Feinde* means "Devils."

4. Convinced that salvation comes from faith alone and not from good works, Boltzius preached unceasingly against self-righteousness (*eigene Gerechtigkeit*) self-piety (*eigene Frömmigkeit*), use of the means of salvation (*Mittel des Heils*) such as church ritual and reputable behavior (*ehrbarer Wandel*). All of these give a person false security (*Sicherheit*) and cause him to fail to depend upon Christ's merits.

5. Boltzius numbers the Sabbath commandment as the third, following Lutheran (and Roman Catholic) numbering. It divides the first commandment into two, thus causing a difference by one in the numbering of the intervening commandments. This translation numbers them according to the Greek system, which is standard in English literature.

6. *Du sollst von deinem Thun lassen ab, dass Gott sein Werck in dir hab'.*

7. For the Pietists, sickness, although harmful to the body, was salutary for the soul, which it properly humbled. The same was true of any physical loss.

8. *Dort wird mein GOtt in ewger Lust aufs schönste mit mir handeln, mein Creutz, das mir und ihm bewusst, in Himmels-Freud verwandeln, da wird mein Weinen lauter Wein, mein Aechzen eitel Freude seyn, das glaub ich, hilf GOtt! Amen.* From a hymn.

FEBRUARY

1. Because Boltzius says *Stangen spalten*, it would appear that these are rail fences, instead of the usual fences of planks, unless fence posts are being split. See end of entry for 21 February.

2. Seeing the advantage of private enterprise, Boltzius had successfully resisted Oglethorpe's efforts to have the Salzburgers work communally.

3. Boltzius seems unaware that the idea of "long lots" had been brought from Central Europe. When Joseph Avery, the English surveyor, tried to resist the Vernonburgers' demand for long lots, they threatened him with bodily harm.

4. At first the redeemed indentured servants, as well as the earlier Salzburgers, had been supplied provisions from the storehouse; but later they, and the fourth Salzburger transport, were given a cash allowance instead.

5. David Züblin, a Swiss from Appenzell, was the father of Johann Joachim Zubly, later an important figure in Georgia.

6. This lack was remedied very shortly.

7. Boltzius is most often quoted as giving practical, rather than moral or religious, arguments against slavery. That is understandable, since he was trying to influence the English authorities, whose interests were primarily practical.

8. Samuel Montaigut (Montague) was a Huguenot merchant in Purysburg who had many dealings with the Salzburgers.

9. After receiving much praise for herding their cattle instead of letting them run free, the Salzburgers finally let their cows roam on the open range like the other settlers.

10. The red wolf, long exstinct in the region but now being reintroduced, was a timid creature.

11. Hans Krüsy, an old Swiss.

12. Capt. William Thomson had brought many Swiss and Germans to Georgia at his own risk.

13. Most men served only till the age of twenty-one. Perhaps this lad had to serve longer to pay the passage of other family members, perhaps members who died more than half way across the Atlantic.

14. These are clearly for a split-rail fence. See Feb., note 1.

15. Like other theologians of his day, Boltzius looked upon the people and events of the Old Testament as precursors, or prefigurations, of people and events in the New. For example, the tree in the Garden of Eden, which caused man's fall, prefigured the cross, on which man was redeemed.

16. David was a prefiguration of Jesus. See note 15, above.

MARCH

1. The letter A. usually designates Augsburg. There seems to have been little reason to disguise that city.

2. See Jan., note 7.

3. These friends were German merchants in Venice in the firm of Schalkhauser, Flügel, and Jastrum.

4. Matthias Kurtz did start a plantation but then died.

5. The word *Ebenezer* was interpreted both as "Stone of Help" and "The Lord hath helped so far." The latter seems the more authentic.

6. This was the "corn-shilling," a subsidy of a shilling on each bushel of corn, beans, or sweet potatoes raised in 1739.

7. It was a custom at the time to send Bible verses as gifts to friends.

8. By "German crops" or "European crops" Boltzius meant wheat, rye, oats, and barley, as opposed to corn, rice, and sweet potatoes.

9. This was a cash allowance for buying provisions. See Feb., note 4.

10. The council consisted of a President and five Assistants. At the time, Col. Stephens was the president.

11. In Pietist parlance, "misery" (*Elend*) meant sin, or "alienation from God."

APRIL

1. These must have been the two disciples on the way to Emmaus in Luke 24:13. Perhaps Boltzius was using a Hebrew or Greek spelling.

2. Canstein Bibles were inexpensive Bibles printed in Halle since 1710 by the Pietist Karl Hildebrandt, Baron of Canstein.

3. See Jan., note 3.

4. See Jan., note 7.

5. In the 18th Century, the word "epilepsy" could connote any type of paroxysm.

6. See Jan., note 7.

7. See note 5, above.

8. Josef Ernst had dislocated a thumb, which could not be reset. Eventually gangrene set in, and the hand had to be amputated at the armpit. The operation, while excruciating, was successful; but the patient died of pneumonia. According to Boltzius, such bodily chastisement saved his soul.

9. See March, note 6.

10. See March, note 8.

11. He should not live under the law of the Old Testament but under the grace of the New. The servant was Martin Herzog.

MAY

1. Abercorn soon became a dependency of Ebenezer and remained a predominantly German area until shortly before the Revolution, when the yeoman farmers sold out to William Knox, a wealthy Englishman who developed a large slave-operated agribusiness.

2. This was Robert Williams, the leader of the Malcontents, or disaffected party in Savannah. He slandered Boltzius by saying that, for the Salzburgers, he was "God, priest, and king."

3. The German word *Person*, although feminine, could refer to a male person. Here the feminine gender is used because most such discussions were with women.

4. "Approval."

5. It was more difficult to disguise the ear marks. The Salzburgers' cattle brands and their cows' earmarks are recorded in the *Cattle Brand Book* in the Georgia Archives in Atlanta.

6. The Lutheran's work ethic derived from Luther's conviction that *laborare* was just as important as *orare*.

7. Ignorant of Pietist dogma. They may have been well instructed in secular or "external" matters such as earning a living.

8. See March, note 3.

9. Friederica Bischoff of Purysburg, nèe Unselt, was the wife of Henry Bishop, an Englishman who had been sent from London as a lad to be Boltzius' servant.

JUNE

1. A reading assignment.

2. *Lobe den HErren, der deinen Stand sichtbar segnet, der aus dem Himmel mit Strömen der Liebe geregnet, dencke daran, was der Allmächtige kan, der dir mit Liebe begegnet.* Stanza 4 of the hymn *Lobe den Herrn, den mächtigen König der Ehren*, by Joachim Neander.

3. A religious tractate by Martin Statius.

4. See note 9, below.

5. Carl Heinrich Bogatzky, *Güldenes Schatz-Kästlein der Kinder GOttes*, Halle, many printings. This was a very popular devotional work.

6. See March, note 3. The Venice firm must have demanded anonymity.

7. *GOtt, der dir täglich alles gibt.*
8. "As many words, as much weight."
9. *Des Herrn Lindners Auszüge aus den Postillen B. Lutheri, Bibeln, Gesang-Bücher und Schatzkästlein).* The "B" is a misprint for "D" (Dr.). For *Schatzkästlein*, see note 5, above.
10. "Her" is of course Mrs. Steiner. Boltzius will sometimes even write "I called on Hans Schmidt, and she said . . . "
11. The Georgia Salzburgers were then corresponding with their kinsmen and countrymen who had found refuge in East Prussia and Lithuania.
12. See note 5, above.
13. Johann Anastasius Freylinghausen, *Geist-reiches Gesangbuch*, Halle 1714 ff.
14. Friederica Maria Gronau.
15. *Hilft er nicht zu jeder Frist, hilft er doch wenns nötig ist,* from an unidentified hymn.
16. Archpriest Schumann was chaplain to the Salzburger exiles in East Prussia.
17. Pastor Breuer was another minister with the Prussian Salzburgers who corresponded with those in Ebenezer.
18. Dr. Schultz was superintendant of schools for the Salzburgers in Lithuania.
19. When the Salzburgers abandoned Old Ebenezer against Oglethorpe's wishes, they had to leave all buildings and lumber behind.
20. Heinrich Melchior Muhlenberg, who had passed through Ebenezer during the previous year, was now in Philadelphia, where manufactured goods were more available.
21. See March, note 8.
22. Col. Stephens' disloyal son Thomas, a leader of the Malcontents in Savannah, was aided by the Ebenezer schoolmaster Ortmann in obtaining signatures on a petition to allow the importation of slaves.

JULY

1. Jonathan Bryan, a South Carolina planter who furnished many cows and horses to the Salzburgers, was a bit of a relgious enthusiast and worked hard to convert his slaves.
2. *Ringe, dass dein Eyfer glühe, und die erste Liebe dich von der gantzen Welt abziehe: halbe Liebe hält nicht Stich.* From *Ringe recht, wenn Gottes Gnade,* by Johann Joseph Winkler.
3. Boltzius is referring to the Swiss and German town of Vernonburg, which Joseph Avery had just surveyed on and north of the White Bluff on the Vernon River south of Savannah.
4. The redemptionists received land and provisions under the condition that they cultivate their land; but many left the farms to their wives and children and sought employment elsewhere, often at neighboring forts.
5. This is clearly Mrs. Sanftleben, the only woman who has lost two children. Urlsperger often deletes names even when the identity is obvious.
6. The Francke Foundation in Halle had provided not only ministers for Ebenezer, but also missionaries for Danish missions in East India. Like Boltzius and Gronau, they, too, sent in regular reports, which were published as the *Der Königlichen Dänischen Missionarien aus Ost-Indien eingesandte Ausführliche Berichte,* Halle 1735 ff.

7. *selbst gemachter Trost* had about the same meaning as *eigene Frömmigkeit and Sicherheit.*" See Jan., note 4.

8. *So wahr sich GOtt im Himmel find't, so wahr bin ich sein trautes Kind, von Sünden los, gantz heilig, voller Gnaden. Er will mein lieber Vater seyn, schliesst mich in seine Vorsorg' ein, beschützet mich vor Unglück, Leid und Schaden.* From a hymn.

9. It is not clear from the records which of the Züblin brothers was then residing in Ebenezer, Ambrosius or Johann Jacob.

10. See May, note 3.

11. By *natürliche Leute* Boltzius seems to mean the Old Adam, the unconverted man.

12. Muhlenberg had preached to the Germans in Savannah when visiting Ebenezer the year before.

13. Her *Welt-Ehrbarkeit, fleischliche Sicherheit,* and *Trost* were the same as the previously mentioned *ehrbare Wandel, Sicherheit, eigene Frömmigkeit,* and *selbstgemachte Trost.* See Jan., note 4.

14. *HErr JEsu, sey mein Hort, Versöhner, HErr und Schild, und führ mich wie du wilt, dein bin ich wie ich bin, nimm mich zu eign hin.* From a hymn.

15. In this case again, *Feinde* probably means "devils." See Jan., note 3.

16. *Ringe recht, wenn GOttes Gnade dich nun ziehet und bekehrt, dass dein Geist sich recht entlade von der Last, die ihn beschwert,* by Johann Joseph Winkler.

17. He means, of course, the cattle disease.

18. See note 6, above.

AUGUST

1. Johannes Arndt, *Vier Bücher vom wahren Christentum,* a massive work of many printings, one of them in Pennsylvania, was the best seller among colonial Germans. August Hermann Francke's *Die Lehre vom Anfang christlichen Lebens,* Halle, 1696, was also very popular.

2. Johann Baptist Homann (1664-1724) and his heirs produced some of the best cartographic engravings of the time. Pastor Schmidt's *Biblischer Medicus,* not identified.

3. A panacea manufactured by Johann Caspar Schauer of Augsburg, which was very popular in Ebenezer and its environs.

4. Johann Vigera, a citizen of Strassburg, conducted the fourth Salzburger transport from London to Georgia. He was now on his way to Philadelphia.

5. When Andreas Zwiffler, the apothecary who came over with the first Salzburger transport, departed for Philadelphia, he left his brandy-still behind. It was inherited by the new physician, Christian Ernst Thilo, who also used it for distilling medications. While backing Oglethorpe in his opposition to rum, Boltzius accepted brandy as a necessary medicine.

6. Bonaventura Riesch, the minister to the Salzburgers who resided in Lindau, continued his interest in them after they came to Ebenezer with the fourth transport.

7. This sackcloth was not for making sacks but for straining the meal.

8. During the first years, Urlsperger succeeded in maintaining a strict censorship of all letters from Ebenezer.

9. Martin Luther's *Haus- und Kirchen Postille über die Evangelia* .

10. The cattle disease (blackwater) reached Ebenezer only after having plagued the surroundings for two years.

11. See Feb., note 3.

12. The city of Hardwick made a start but soon joined the other "dead towns of Georgia."

13. Luther has *Lehre uns bedenken, dass wir sterben müssen* , which is very direct. The King James version has "So teach us to number our days."

14. In King James this is Jonah 2:8. Luther renders it as *Die über dem Nichtigen halten, verlassen ihre Gnade.*

SEPTEMBER

1. Jeremias Theus, a Swiss, later painted Boltzius' portrait.

2. Thomas Causton had been replaced as keeper of the stores in Savannah and was about to go to London to have his accounts audited.

3. This is an early example of share-cropping, which was later to harm Georgia's agriculture.

4. The Salzburgers had to wait until 1749, when Capt. Peter Bogg brought a transport of Palatines on the *Charles Town Galley.*

5. *Ach GOtt! du bist noch heut so reich, als du bist gewesen ewiglich.* From a hymn.

6. *Mein Vertrauen steht gantz zu dir; mach mich an meiner Seelen reich, so hab ich genug hier und ewiglich.* From a hymn.

7. *Thue als ein Kind und lege dich in deines Vaters Arme, bitte ihn und flehe, bis er sich dein, wie er pflegt, erbarme, so wird er dich durch seinen Geist auf Wegen, die du ietzt nicht weisst, nach wohlbehaltnem Ringen aus allen Sorgen bringen.* From a hymn.

8. Boltzius writes Leckner. The name also appears as Lechner and Lackner, which seems to have been the name that prevailed.

9. Boltzius seems to have used the word *Schindeln* to mean not only shingles but also weatherboards, which it probably means here.

10. Boltzius uses the word *Stube* (cognate with Eng. *stove*) for the heated room and the word *Kammer* for the bedroom, even though that word (cognate with Lat. *camina*) originally meant a heated room.

11. Kitchens were usually built separate from the house as a precaution against fire.

12. Although the stove was in the room, it was fed from outside so one did not have to enter the room with dirty shoes and dirty firewood. The stove pipe also emptied outside, thus keeping smoke out of the room.

13. Cards were a sort of curry comb for carding wool or flax.

14. There is a kind of polecat in Germany (*Iltis*), but nothing to compare in stench with an American skunk.

15. This Old Testament verse is perhaps the best support for the Pietists' belief that sickness is salutary.

16. For the meaning of "secure" (*sicher*), see Jan., note 3.

17. Although Salzburg was a part of the Holy Roman Empire, when a person left there he was going "into the Empire."

OCTOBER

1. When the first Salzburger exiles reached Augsburg, they were quartered in the Evangelical poorhouse.

2. See June, note 5.

3. For *True Christianity* see Aug., note 1. *Ehre und Lehre Augsburgischer Confession* and *Tractätlein von der Bekehrung* unidentified.

4. Christian and Margaretha Löwenberger, who had come over with Capt. William Thomson in 1738, had been indentured to the schoolmaster Ortmann; but he had been unable to maintain them and they were returned to the service of the Trustees.

5. *Moses hat nun ausregieret, Christi freyer Geist uns führet, die Gefangenschaft ist aus; wer gehört in Gottes Haus, kan durch unsers Goels Büssen, freyer Kindschaft nun geniessen. Hallelujah!,* from the hymn *Auf, Auf, weil der Zag erschienen,* by J.A. Freylinghausen.

6. "Memory aid." From *adminiculum,* a beanpole, support.

NOVEMBER

1. The Kieffer girl's name is not given. It may have been Ottile, born in 1728.

2. There having been no one by the name of Stocher in Ebenezer, this must have been a typographical error for Mrs. Thomas Bacher.

3. *Glauchisches Gedenck-Büchlein, Oder Einfältiger Unterricht für die Christliche Gemeinde zu Glaucha,* Leipzig and Halle, 1693. Glaucha, the seat of the Francke Foundation, is now in Halle but was then a neighboring village.

4. Since there was no one named Stichler at Ebenezer, this must have been an error for Bichler.

5. Boltzius is probably distinguishing between long leaf and short leaf pine.

DECEMBER

1. Orangeburg was a township on the South Carolina frontier settled by Swiss and Germans. By Boltzius' standards, it was a wild and godless place. Besides that, it was Reformed rather than Lutheran.

2. Although Urlsperger suppressed Steiner's name at the beginning of this entry, he failed to do so here.

Index

Aaron, Pastor, convert in India 80

Abercorn, village near juncture of Abercorn Creek and Savannah River *passim;* May, note 1

Abercorn Creek (Mill River), branch of Savannah River ii, 13, 65

Agriculture, see crops.

Arndt, Johann, author of *True Christianity* 89, 115; Aug., note 1

Arnold, Gottfried, hymnist 130

Arnsdorff, Peter, Palatine, learning blacksmithing 105

Arnsdorf, Sophia, Palatine, converses with Boltzius 7

Avery, Joseph, English surveyor, completes work 97, 98; Feb., note 3, July note 3

Augusta, city up Savannah River, mentioned 16

Augsburg, city in Swabia, benefactors in 61, gifts from 62, 112, 113, poorhouse in 111

Ausführliche Nachrichten, Urlsperger's edition of the Ebenezer reports ii; Jan. note 1

Bacher, Christina, Salz, wid Matthäus, in good spiritual state 80

Bacher, Maria, Salz, w Thomas, sick 4, prepares for Holy Communion 110

Baptisms, importance of 25; see Births and Baptisms.

Bears, destroy livestock 15

Benefactions: from Augsburg and Halle 112, 114, for Boltzius' house 187

Biblischer Medicus, medical exegesis 90; Aug., note 2

Bichler, see Pichler.

Births and baptisms, in 1742 p. 1; in 1743, Theobald Kieffer, Jr. 2, Sanftleben 23, twins in Savannah 60, Gronau 67

Bischoff, see Bishop.

Bishop, Friederica, Palatine, nee Unselt, w Henry sick in orphanage 56; May, note 9

Blacksmiths, see Smiths.

Blackwater, see Cattle disease

Bogatzky, Carl Heinrich, Pietist author; June, note 5

Books, donation of 112, 114

Boltzius, Johann Martin, pastor at Ebenezer ii and *passim*

Bounty, see Corn-shilling.

Breuer, Pastor, chaplain to Salzburgers in East Prussia 68

Bricks, lack of 16

Bridge and causeway, building of 102

Bruckner, Georg, Salz, visits Boltzius 41, 42, serves as locksmith 104

Bryan, Jonathan, South Carolina planter, letter from 75, letter to 80; July, note 1

Buchfelder, Ernst Wilhelm, hymnist 129

Butcher 38

Cadzand, place in Holland 100

Canstein Bible 37; April, note 2

Catholics, soldier converts 89

Cattle, driven into forest 15, requested for 4th transport 35, 39, run loose 46, 50, sent by Causton 50, given to indentured servants and 4th transport 69, bought from Dr. Graham 69

Cattle Brand Book May, note 5

Cattle disease iii, at White Bluff 78, at Ebenezer 79, 83, 84, 89, 93, 96, 98; Feb., note 9, July, note 17, Aug., note 10

Causton, Thomas, keeper of the stores in Savannah, sends cattle 50, brings news 100; Sept., note 2

Cedar, see Trees

Cellar, needed for Ludwig Meyer 105

Charcoal 104

Christ, Gottfried, converted Jew, ill 87

Churches, see Jerusalem and Zion.

Communal labor 12, 18, 81

Confirmation 34

Consecration, see house consecration.

Construction, see Church, Mill.

Continuations, the continuations of the *Ausführliche Nachrichten*

Corn-shilling, subsidy on crops 29, 30, 45, 101; March, note 6

Cotton, see Crops.

Council, governing body in Savannah, consisting of a President and five Assistants

Cows, see Cattle.

Crops: barley 45, 91, beans 94, 107, 110, corn 45, 94, 107, cotton 118, oats 91, peanuts 107, peas 110, rice 13, 45, rye 91, squash 107, sweet potatoes 107, wheat 45, 70, 90. See Grapes, Vegetables.

Cypress, see Trees.

Deaths, in 1742, p. 1; in 1743: Sanftleben twins 23, woman from Purysburg 74, unnamed infant 119, Matthias Kurtz 122

Depp, . . . , bro Anna Elisabetha Kieffer 127

Diseases: "epilepsy" 43, April, note 7; tertian fever 113

Dogma of the Beginning of Christian Life 89; Aug., note 1

Drought 65, ends 67, 72

East India, missionary reports from 88

East Prussia, see Prussia.

Ebenezer, Salzburger settlement near Savannah i and *passim*, origin of name 27; March note 5; census of inhabitants 104

Ebenezer Creek, unnavigable waterway from Old to New Ebenezer i, plantations on 36, 38, 42

Ehre und Lehre Augsburgischer Confession, religious tract 115; Oct., note 3

Eischberger, David, Salz, miller, visited by Boltzius 82, loses cow 96

Eischberger, Catharina, Salz, w David, visited by Boltzius 82

English boy dies at Ebenezer 121

English manager at Old Ebenezer 6, 47

Ernst, Josef, deceased h of Anna Maria, mentioned 43; April, note 8

"Fathers," Salzburger patrons. See G.A. Francke, Urlsperger, Ziegenhagen.

Fences: split rails 12, 17–19, 26; Feb., note 1; downed by storm 72

Fever, see Disease.

Flerl, Carl, Salz, visited by Boltzius 78

Flerl, Hans, bro Carl, Salz, cuts boards 22, 123, yearns for heaven 88, likes religious text 92, keeping legacy 99

Flerl, Maria, nee Gruber, w Carl, has fever 4

Fourth Salzburger Transport, cattle and provisions for 35

Francke, August Hermann, founder of Francke Foundation in Halle, book by 121

Francke, Gotthilf August, s A. G. Francke, letters from, 24, 90, forwards gift 68

Francke Foundation (Franckesche Stiftungen), charitable institution in Halle ii; July, note 6

Frederica, British outpost near Florida, mentioned 50

Freylinghausen Hymnbook, favorite hymnal at Ebenezer, printed at Halle in many editions 67

Freylinghausen, Johann Anastasius, professor at Halle, composer 116, 129; June, note 13

Fritzsch, Ahasverus, hymnist 129

Fruit, needs rain 65: apples 73, grapes, being planted 10, 73, peaches 73, 81, for brandy 73, 91

Funerals, nature of 123

Gerhardt, Paul, hymnist 130, 130

German crops iii; March, note 8

Germans in Savannah, some calum-
niate Ebenezer 6, receive diet
money 12, collect money for
church in Philadelphia 83, 93,
mentioned 92, divine services 48,
70, 89, 93, 122. See Vernonburg.
Glaner, Georg, Salz, visited by
Boltzius 37
Glaner, Gertraut, Salz, nee Lemmenhoffer, w Georg, leaves orphanage 106
Glaucha, site of Francke Foundation,
now in Halle 121; Nov., note 3
Glauchisches Gedenckbüchlein, religious
tract 121; Nov., note 3
The Glory and Dogma of the Augsburg
Confession, see Ehre und Lehre.
Graham, Dr., wealthy English neigh-
bor 50, brands Salzburgers' cattle
68, sells cows 69
Graniwetter, Anna Catharina, Salz,
w Caspar, witnesses God's blessing
106
Grapes, see Fruit.
Grass (crab grass), burned off 14, al-
most ineradicable 11, 71
Gronau, Friederica Maria, infant
daughter of Israel Chr., born 67
Gronau, Israel Christian, assistant
minister in Ebenezer ii and passim
Haberfehner, Magdalena, deceased
Austrian child 7
Halle, East German city, home of
Francke Foundation, source of
gifts 61–63, 65
Haslocher, Johann Adam, hymnist
129
Hay 12, 18, 37
Hedinger, Johann Reinhold, hymn-
ist 130
Heinrich, Anna Magdalena, Pal-
atine, marries Ott 17
Herrnschmidt, Johann Daniel,
hymnist 130
Hertzog, Martin, Salz, servant at or-
phanage 94; April, note 11
Hildebrandt, Carl, Baron of Can-
stein, publisher of Bibles; April,
note 2

Hoes, inefficient and exhausting 71,
104
Holy Communion 34, 41, 61, 89,
110; Sept., note 17
Homann, Johann Baptist, engraver
of maps 90; Aug., note 2
Holy Roman Empire 110; Sept., note
17
Horse collars, lent by Jones 91
Horses, to be grazed 17, brood
mares 91
House and Church Postille, text by
Martin Luther 65, 92; June, note
9, Aug., note 9
House consecrations: Simon Reiter
32, Kornberger 33
Hymns, see Appendix I
Indentured servants, to be brought
at expense of Trustees 101, provi-
sioned; Feb., note 4, July, note 4;
provisions for indentured servants
at Ebenezer 33, need of 125
India, missions in 80; July, note 6
Jerusalem Church, town church in
Ebenezer 45, origin of name 27,
distribution at 63, linen for 92,
Christmas at 126
Jones, Thomas, keeper of the stores
in Savannah, receives Boltzius 28,
47, relates anecdote 30, lends
house 48, going to Frederica 50,
letters from 74, 76, lends horse
collars 91
Kalcher, Margaret, Salz, w.
Ruprecht, grows seeds 90, receives
books 93
Kalcher, Ruprecht, Salz, manager of
orphanage, grazes horses 17, men-
tioned 79, 89, uses plow 91, plants
crops 94, prays 96, receives letter
117
Kehl, Johann Georg, hymnist 129
Kendal, Duchess of, benefactress 107
Kieffer, Anna Elisabetha, nee Depp,
Palatine, w Johann Jacob 127
Kieffer, Anna Margaretha, mother-
in-law of Maria, sick 1
Kieffer, (Johann) Jacob, Palatine, s
Theobald, Sr. 127

Kieffer, Maria, nee Bacher, w Theo Jr., sick 1, 2, 7, in fine spirits 80, contented 110, edifying 116

Kieffer, Theobald, Sr., Palatine from Purysburg, wishes to move to Ebenezer 44, buys Ludwig Mueller's house 105

Kieffer, Theobald, Jr., s Theobald, 2, land flooded 14, loses boards 22, edifying 116, cutting boards 123

Klocker, Bernhard, Salz, leaves legacy 99

Kogler, Georg, Salz, chief carpenter, to move to orphanage 106, 111

Kornberger (Cornberger), Johann, Salz, builds and consecrates house 33

Knox, William, wealthy Englishman; May, note 1

Krusy, Hans, Swiss from Purysburg, works for wages 15, 37; Feb., note 11

Kurtz, Matthias, Salzburger from Cadzant, arrives 23, visited by Boltzius 93, receives plantation 100, sick 119, dies 122

Lackner, Catharina Barbara, Salz, nee Ulmer, w Martin II, making good progress 43, a good example 74

Lackner, Margaretha, Salz, w Martin, speaks with Boltzius 35, making progress 43

Lackner, Martin I, Salz of 3rd transport, sells tools 104; Sept. note 8

Lackner, Martin II, Salz of 4th transport, present at prayer 74, to help Kalcher 100

Lackner girl, gives twill 28

Legacies: see Klocker, Schmidt, Schweighoffer.

Leimberger (Lemberger), Christian, Salz, molested by skunk 107

Leitner, Josef, Salz, established as smith 104

Lemberger, see Leimberger

Lemmenhofer, Veit, Salz, speaks to Boltzius 43, to help orphans 71

Linder, Superintendant, author 60, 65

Lithuania see Prussia.

Little Treasure Chest (Güldenes Schatzkästlein der Kinder Gottes), devotional book by Carl Heinrich Bogatzky 60, 65, 67, 115

Lochner, Carl Friedrich, hymnist 130

Locksmiths, see Bruckner, Schrempf.

Long lots; Feb., note 3

Loewenberger (Lewenberger), Christian, Palatine in Savannah 115; Oct., note 4

London, source of gifts 61

Lumber: boards burn 22, boards at Old Ebenezer given 69

Luther, Martin, German reformer, quoted 40, mentioned 60, author of Postille 65, 92, hymnist 129; May, note 6, June, note 9, Aug., notes 9, 13, 14

Malaria, see Disease.

Marriages in 1742, p. 1; in 1743: Otto-Heinrich 17

Medicines, from Halle 4, 7, 112, 113: theriac 116, Schauer Balm 90, 116

Memorial and Thanksgiving Feast, celebrated 24

Metzger, Jacob, Palatine from Purysburg, father of Mrs. Christ, sick 120

Meyer, Elisabeth, w Johann Ludwig, donates twill 28

Meyer, (Johann) Ludwig, physician with 4th Salz trans, his house completed 104, 105, sells old house 105

Midwives, see Maria Rheinlander.

Mill, being repaired 70, 81

Mill River, see Abercorn Creek.

Montague, Samuel, deceased Huguenot merchant in Purysburg 13; Feb., note 8

Muhlenberg, Heinrich Melchior, pastor from Halle, asks question 27, letter from 70, letter to 71, sends psalm 73, loved by Savannah Germans 83, correspondence with 90, 121; June, note 20, July, note 12

Mulberry trees, see Trees.

Müller, Joseph Theodor, hymnist 129

Neander, Joachim, hymnist 130

Negroes, a burden 13, live badly at Port Royal 31, baptized 75, 80; Oglethorpe opposed to introduction of 100

Newman, Henry, secretary of SPCK, letter from 54

Ogeechee River, blackwater stream parallel lower reches of Savannah River, mentioned 97

Oglethorpe, James Edward, founder of Georgia, pleased with name of Ebenezer 27, has barony 15, 73 letter from 28, gives wine 47, to return to London 74, 76, promoted to general 76

Old Ebenezer, first location of Salzburgers, now the Trustees' cowpen i, lumber at 69; June, note 19

Orangeburg, German and Swiss settlement in South Carolina 127; Dec., note 1

Orphanage, mentioned 54, 56, 98, overcrowded 99, well being repaired 107

Ortmann, Christoph, schoolmaster, joins plot 73, takes in English boy 121; June, note 22, Oct., note 4

Orton, Christopher, Anglican minister in Savannah, refugee at Ebenezer 117

Ott, Carl Sigismund, Salz, marries Anna Magdalena Heinrich 17

Painting, allegorial, sent to Vigera 95

Palachacolas, a small fort up the Savannah River from Ebenezer 15

Pichler, Margaretha, nee Kieffer, w Thomas, mentioned 58, 118, attends engagement 118

Pichler, Thomas, Salz, recognizes sins 58, attends engagement 118

Pietist terminology, iii; Jan., notes 3, 4, 7, March, note 11, May, note 7, July, notes 7, 11, 13

Pine forests, praise of 71, 72

Plows, introduction of iii, needed 71, 104, 124, used by Kalcher 91

Port Royal, small port in South Carolina, mentioned 14, 31, 46

Postille, see House and Church Postille.

President, see Council.

Prussia and Lithuania, refuge of Salzburger exiles 66, 68

Purysburg, Swiss settlement across and down river from Ebenezer ii and passim; patients from 54, 56, daughter dies 74, mother still sick 98

Radishes, see Vegetables.

Reiter, Simon, Salz, consecrates house 32

Rheinlander, Maria, Palatine, wid Friedrich, midwife 23

Rice, see Crops.

Rice stamping machine, needed 13, 70, to be built 81

Richter, Christian Friedrich, hymnist 129

Riesch, Rev. Bonaventura, clergyman in Lindau, sends linen 51, 92; Aug., note 6

Rieser, Bartholomäus, Salz, ill 53

Rieser, Michael, Salz, son of Bartholomäus, sick 25, 85, 87

Rieser, Simon, Salz, invalid, recuperates 108

Rinkert, Martin, hymnist 130

Riser, see Rieser.

Road construction 101

Saalfeld, German city, benefactors in 61

Sabbath violated 6

Salt, bought in Savannah 84

Sanftleben, Georg, Silesian carpenter, poor crop 9

Sanftleben, Magdalena, nee Arnsdorff, Palatine, w Georg, bears daughter 23; July, note 5

Savannah, chief city in Georgia, passim

Savannah River, plantations on 101

Schalkhauser, Fluegel, and Jastrum, merchants in Venice, send money for Kurtz family 23, letter from 54, benefactors 55, 61; July, note 5

Schatzkästlein, see Little Treasure Chest.

Schauer, Johann Caspar, manufacturer of balm 116; Aug., note 3

Schauer's balm, see Medicines.

Scheraus, Johann, receives letter 85

Schmidt, Johann (Hans), Austrian, offers gift to church 28

Schmidt, Johann Eusebius, hymnist 130

Schmidt, Pastor, author of *Biblisher medicus* 90

Schoolmasters, see Christoph Ortmann, Ruprecht Steiner.

Schrempf, Ruprecht, Salz, locksmith 104, proposes to Kieffer girl 117–118, buys tools from Lackner 104, lacks sheet iron 125

Schultz, Dr., superintendant of Salzburger schools in East Prussia 68

Schumann, Archpriest, chaplain to the Salzburgers in East Prussia 68

Schwartzwälder, Johann, Palatine redemptioner from Old Ebenezer, blamed iii, redeemed 3, ill 82

Schwarzwälder, Mrs., Pal fr Old Ebenezer, bitten by snake 75

Schweighoffer, Margaretha, nee Pindlinger, Salz, wid, now weak 9, legacy 9, recuperates 127

Second hand clothes, sold in Savannah 21

Servants (hired hands), see Indentured servants.

Shoemakers: Zettler,

Sickbay, planned 70

Silk culture, a beginning made 31–32, 39

Singing lessons 126

Smiths, see Leitner, Peter Arnsdorf.

Snakebite: Mrs. Schwartzwälder 75

Society, see SPCK.

Spanish invasion, recalled 20, 29, 62, 64, 66, 82, 109, 117

SPCK (Society for the Promotion of Christian Knowledge), missionary society in London, sends still for peach brandy 91

Statii Lutherus Ridivivus, religious text by Martin Statius 60

Steiner, Maria, Salz, nee Winter, w Ruprecht, eyes are opened 127

Steiner, Ruprecht, Salz, speaks to Boltzius 29, 127, converses edifyingly 51, 53, receives information 60, digs well 65, inclined to give boards 70

Stephens, Thomas, s Col. Stephens, leader of Malcontents 73; June, note 22

Stephens, Col. Wm., Trustees' secretary in Georgia, pleased that servants are settling 5, gives vine cuttings 10, sending corn 47, requests names 104; March, note 10

Stills, for brandy needed 73, donated 91

Stricker, ———, German in Savannah, bears heavy cross 83

Stricker, Mrs. ———, woman in Savannah 83

Surinam, South American colony, mentioned 14

Tavern, established at Ebenezer 123

Theriac, see Medicines.

Theus, Jeremias, Swiss painter in Charleston 100; Sept., note 1

Thilo, Christian Ernst, physician, lends laboratory still 91

Thomson, Capt. William, mariner 17; Feb., note 12, Oct., note 4

Treasure Chest, see *Little Treasure Chest*.

Trees: cedar 15–16, cypress 16, 123, mulberry 32, oak 71, 72, walnut 71, 72

True Christianity (Wahres Christentum), see Arndt.

Trustees for Establishing a Colony in Georgia *passim*

Turnips, see vegetables

Urlsperger, Samuel, Senior of Lutheran ministry in Augsburg ii, letter from 22

Vegetables, growing well 45, 90, need rain 65: chard 90, head cabbage 90, kohlrabi 90, squash 107, turnips 8

Venice, see Schalkhauser.

Vernonburg, Swiss and German town on Vernon River 12, cattle disease there 78, description of 94: July, note 3, has long lots; Feb., note 3, beginning poorly 77, crops improve 94

Vigera, Johann, citizen of Strassburg, conductor of 4th Salzburger transport, reaches Port

Royal 31, to buy plows 91, his jour-
ney commended 92, receives alle-
gorical painting 95, sends
newspapers 106, in Pennsylvania
125; Aug., note 4
Vines, see Grapes.
War of Jenkins' Ear, see Spanish
invasion.
Watson, . . . , alderman in Savannah
Wells, abundant water 99, well at or-
phanage repaired 107, Steiner
digs well 65
Wheat, see crops.
White Bluff, same as Vernonburg
Williams, Robert, leader of the Mal-
contents 46; May, note 2
Wills, see legacies.
Winkler, Johann Joseph, hymnist
130
Wolves, destructive 15; Feb., note 10
Zant, Bartholomäus, Swiss, visited by
Boltzius 37
Zettler (Zedler, Zetler), Matthias,
Salz, shoemaker, takes Depp as ap-
prentice 127

Ziegenhagen, Friedrich Michael,
royal chaplain, "Reverend Father"
of the Georgia Salzburgers, letters
from 62, 107, to send painting 96
Zimmerebner, Ruprecht, Salz, to aid
orphanage 71
Zion Church, church on plantations,
being constructed 19, services at
26, 55, 77, origin of name 27, receives linen 51, 92, mentioned 75,
123
Zubli, Ambrosius, Swiss, bro of Joh.
Jac. One of the two at Ebenezer
82; July, note 9
Zublin, David, bro of Ambrosius, father of Johann Joachim 13; Feb.,
note 5
Zublin, Johann Jacob, see Zubli,
Ambrosius.
Zwiffler, Andreas, apothecary with
first transport, receives still 91;
Aug., note 5